National Book Award Finalist

"Riveting true story about the author's life on a sailboat with her young family. Sensitive, brave, inspiring, funny, and beautifully written—you won't be able to put it down! Reveals how the author comes to find herself through love, loss, raising a child at sea, and her fears and joys."

—Helena Dea Bala
Author of *Craigslist Confidential*

"Most cruising yarns are written by men, for men, and only mention the reluctant spouse reluctantly. Not 'Holding Fast.' It is a lyrical tale of a young woman (and mother) learning the ropes—of her floating home, her marriage, and life itself."

—Cap'n Fatty Goodlander of *Cruising World* magazine

"Thoroughly absorbing... Vivid story of survival and adaptation that operates on many different levels, promising to attract not just readers of true-life adventure, but those who want stories of endurance and moving forward...Enlightening, moving."

—D. Donovan, Senior Reviewer, *Midwest Book Review*

"A wife follows her husband to sea and finds herself along the way in this memoir... A perfect, realistic counterpart to Amity Gaige's *Sea Wife* (2020), Cole's moving memoir is emotionally astute, and her use of excerpts from the *Laughing Goat's* log provides welcome insights into John's perspective. Vivid characterizations... The author's voice is so assured..."

—*Kirkus Reviews*

"Susan Cole's honest and poignant memoir is an adventure story and love letter wrapped in one. Holding fast can require letting go, and for Cole, following her husband's dream to sail away leads her to discover unknown strengths within herself, and everything she needs to make it home. A heartwarming read."

—Jennifer Rosner
Author of *The Yellow Bird Sings*

HOLDING FAST

A Memoir of Sailing, Love, and Loss

Susan Cole

2021 White Bird Publications

Copyright © 2021 by Susan Cole

Published in the United States
by White Bird Publication, LLC, Texas

Paperback ISBN 978-1-63363-537-1
eBook ISBN 978-1-63363-538-8
Library of Congress Control Number 2021945440

Cover design by Benedetta C. Vialli
Author Photo by Jessica Donley
Map by Raegan Russell

PRINTED IN THE UNITED STATES OF AMERICA

To John and Kate

FAIRFIELD
CT
NORFOLK
INTRACOASTAL WATERWAY
MIAMI
The Bahamas
ISLAMUJER
Yucatan
CA
MOHO CAYE
Barrier Reef
BELIZE
RIO DULCE
Guatemala
HONDURAS

ORIDA
MIAMI
NASSAU
KEY WEST
HAVANA
THE BAHAMAS
CUBA
BEAN
A
JAMAICA
N

Table of Contents

HOLDING FAST

A Memoir of Sailing, Love, and Loss

White Bird Publications

No, I'd never been to this country

before. No, I didn't know where the roads

would lead me. No, I didn't intend to

turn back.

—MARY OLIVER, *FELICITY*

Felicity by Mary Oliver, Published by The Penguin Press New York
Copyright © 2015 by Mary Oliver
Reprinted by permission of The Charlotte Sheedy Literary Agency Inc.

Chapter One
Underway

We still lived in Connecticut that Saturday my husband, John, and I took our seven-year-old daughter Kate to Mystic Seaport. As we reached the town of white picket fences and tidy window boxes of petunias, geraniums, and zinnias, John turned to Kate and said, "In a few weeks, we're going to move on *Laughing Goat* and go sailing."

I sprang to attention in the back. We had discussed breaking the news to Kate, but I hadn't known when John would do it. He waited until we came under the spell of the tall ships and recreated nineteenth-century village where blacksmiths and carpenters plied their trades. As usual, John took his time, raising a cigarette to his lips, inhaling, flicking ash in the tiny metal tray, flashing a grin at me, and waiting for Kate's response. Though the smell of his cigarette smoke no longer intoxicated me as it had twenty years ago, I still loved the sensual curve of John's hand around a cigarette.

John was six when his family moved to Africa. Before

they went, his mother told him about lions and tigers and elephants and snakes, anthills as big as houses, and the wild bush that would surround their new house where he could play. He couldn't wait to go. He wanted to impart a similar excitement to Kate about our voyage.

"Where are we going?" Kate asked.

"South. First to Florida. Then we'll figure out where we want to go from there—somewhere in the Caribbean. We'll snorkel. There are fantastic coral reefs, like nothing you've ever seen."

"What about school?"

"You and Mom will do it on the boat."

"What about our house?"

"We'll rent it out."

Kate glanced at me. Passing the schooners on Mystic River, I could imagine sailing down the Intracoastal Waterway through charming towns like those on Long Island Sound.

"It'll be fun," I said, feeling like Judas. I didn't share my doubts and fears.

Kate told her class the next day that she was sailing to the Caribbean and snorkeling, and she wasn't going to school anymore. Her teacher, a sailor, was thrilled for her and asked her to write the class about her adventures. She promised they would write back.

I wish it had been that simple for me. I did not want to go. John would tease me and say, "I'll have to drag you out kicking and screaming, clinging to the garden." I imagined myself red-faced and shrieking, my fingers black with dirt, while John yanked my legs and Kate stared open-mouthed.

I was not a person who yelled. John wasn't, either. In our twenties vacationing in Isla Mujeres, Mexico, I was surprised when one of the locals with whom we convivially joked at a bar described us as the "quiet couple." There was so much feeling between us that we never felt quiet to me. From the outside, though, we appeared so.

We, us. When we fell in love, I glommed onto John as

though he would save my life. He glommed onto me, too, as a way out of roles that smothered: husband and father at eighteen, John Jr. to his dad's John Sr., the inherited mantle of a family who sailed to America on the *Mayflower*. The youngest of four, with three older sisters, he was "irresponsible John" in his family, a party boy and artist in high school who beat to his own drum.

I, too, was the baby in my family, arriving nine years after my sister and eleven after my brother. A much unexpected, unplanned third child. The four were already a family, locked in one argument after another, instigated by my volatile mother. My dad was the only one who lit up when I came into a room. I learned to stay under the radar, to feel out the temperature before I ventured a word. In audiotapes my mother recorded of our family dinners, mine was the high voice piping up, "Shut up and listen." My dad died of heart disease when I was ten, and I was lost until I met John.

John and I lived in our house in Fairfield for nearly ten years, and Kate had lived there her whole life. Before that, John and I lived on old wooden boats in Long Island Sound for fifteen years. On the water, we had no address.

Our address on land, 425 Brookside Drive, sounded so solid, a red farmhouse on a hill alongside the Mill River and a nature conservancy from which deer would thunder out of early morning mists. At first, I would repeat the address over and over, pinching myself as I wandered through the house on polished hardwood floors and flung open the tall casement windows.

I wasn't ready to give the house up to live out John's dream of sailing off. As we sailed, the house became a beacon for me, the cozy red house on a hill, lights twinkling from the windows, river gurgling, the smell of wild strawberries drifting through the air, and a tattered tire swing suspended from a maple tree that Kate and her friends swung on over the stream, waiting for our return.

Now many years later, John has passed away, and the voyage occupies a space in my mind as bright as the lights of Havana when we drifted outside the harbor waiting for daylight to enter, but I can no longer ask him what he thinks it all meant.

Chapter Two
Dream

John and I met at an offbeat company in Greenwich, Connecticut, in 1969 that attracted college graduates eager to avoid real jobs. On my first day, decked out in a minidress and white fishnet stockings, I introduced myself to John, twenty-four, in the office next to mine. I was twenty-two, with long, wavy chestnut hair, light blue eyes, and a small, round face. John's eyes were a piercing deep blue, and his blond hair was tucked behind his ears. His face was large and square-jawed. He wore jeans, leather sandals, and a white linen Nehru shirt. On the walls around his desk, he had pinned up children's drawings and a black-and-white photograph of a naked, curly-haired little girl in a field of daisies. He stared at me while taking a drag on a cigarette. He didn't say anything.

I asked him about the photo. It was his five-year-old daughter, who also made the drawings. He must have married even earlier than I had at nineteen.

We were assigned to work on a project together. I sat on the floor in his office, my legs tucked under me, as he paced around and smoked. When I asked a question, he didn't answer right away. His pauses flustered me. He took a moment, rested his chin on his palm, smoked a cigarette, and stared into the distance or at me, while I pulled at my sweater and fidgeted. I wasn't used to people thinking about what I said.

We got to know one another. I found out that he learned to sail at the age of four. His English and Scottish ancestors were ministers and university provosts. He grew up in Greenwich but spent part of his childhood in Africa, where his dad, a metallurgical engineer, opened up a copper mine. Supporting a wife and child, John took seven years to graduate from college while working as a sailmaker and baby photographer. I zipped through college in three years and then got a master's degree. John wanted to buy a boat when he had enough money.

He asked, "Have you ever sailed?"

I laughed. I wasn't athletic. No one I knew sailed. I grew up in landlocked Ohio. My Jewish immigrant family prized education, not sports. I had a tenuous connection to the water through my parents, who emigrated with their families on crowded ships in the early 1900s to escape persecution in Eastern Europe and Russia, but John talked about the Bermuda Race, a three-day sail from New York, that he had always wanted to do. I imagined sails flying in the wind as a green island with tiny pink houses shimmered in the distance.

John teased me mercilessly. I came to work one day in a blond wig and slinked around the office like Marilyn Monroe, fishing for compliments. My boss praised my sexy look. When John saw me, he chortled. Until that moment, I thought I looked great. A few minutes later, John came into my office and stuck a paper bag over my head.

"Ha!" I think now, more than forty years later. "That's

John." At the time, it startled me. I hardly knew him, but he saw me differently than others did, or than I saw myself.

He admired Diane Arbus, Richard Avedon, Andy Warhol, Janis Joplin, the Rolling Stones. His icons tested cultural boundaries, which made me uncomfortable. I liked Impressionist paintings, Russian novelists, and Simon and Garfunkel.

Over wine-fueled lunches with our colleagues in the early 1970s, we discussed peace marches, the draft, Woodstock, and Richard Nixon. We had all married young, and the heady new freedom in the air stirred desire and longing.

I met my first husband, a medical student whom I was supporting through medical school, in college. When he discovered that he hated the sight of blood, he quit med school to become an IBM salesman. I wasn't sure what to make of his betrayal of our future.

Then, one day when he came home after work, he said, "I have to be honest. I've had an affair with someone I met during training." Since then, when I hear, "I have to be honest," I brace myself. That night after I yelled at him and cried, I lay on my side of the bed watching him raise the windows precisely one inch so he could sleep, and I questioned what I ever saw in him. I began therapy.

At work, my friendship with John deepened. I draped myself over a chair in his office, and we talked for hours, mostly about sailing. His sailing stories captivated me.

The daydream went on and on until, two years later, I left that company for a market research job near Croton-on-Hudson, New York. I missed John terribly. Every day he called me from his office, or I called him.

One day, we met for lunch. Wrapped in a purple woolen *ruana,* I sat across the table, trying to contain the onslaught of emotion overtaking me. John stared at me through wisps of cigarette smoke. After lunch, we took a walk in the woods to talk about our feelings. Our hands touched, and we pulled together. Then we couldn't keep our hands off each other—

in his office, in the car, in the park.

I left my husband and rented an apartment on the second floor of a house in Croton-on-Hudson, where I could glimpse the Hudson River through cherry trees whose limbs brushed against the windowpanes. John came over every night and left for home around midnight. I began writing, tapping away on the typewriter as cherry blossoms drifted in through the open windows.

It was hard for John to make up excuses to his wife for his absence each night. I ignored his discomfort. I liked how things were going. I didn't want to make another decision.

He kept bringing up his difficulty. I casually mentioned what he said to my psychoanalyst in Manhattan, whom I was now seeing four days a week.

Dr. R. said, "Does he want to move in with you?"

"Yes."

"How do you feel about that?"

"I'm not sure. I like the way it is."

"He is implying that he would leave his wife and children for you. This is huge. Do you understand that?" The usually soft-spoken Dr. R. practically shouted.

Silence filled the room again.

"I love him," I whispered, tears running down my cheeks.

"Yes?"

"I don't know if he'll stay."

Up to that point, I hadn't acknowledged the strength of my feelings for John. Despite my happiness as I danced around my apartment singing off-key to the cherry trees, the warmth that spread like mellow wine through my body when he was with me, the feeling of my life sliding into place in a way that I remembered from when my dad was alive, I tried to ignore my feelings. I had pushed them aside for so long, and my mother called frequently to draw me into her sphere where the fledgling feelings for John had no place.

John met my mother when he helped me move my belongings out of the garden apartment I shared with my first husband in Scarsdale into my new apartment in Croton-on-Hudson. Uninvited, my mother had popped in for a visit the weekend I was moving out. When John walked in, he said, "Hello, Marion," and she didn't correct him as she usually would: "That's Meriam with an e," in a loud, bright voice with a fake smile. She seemed a little afraid of him.

John and I escaped into the apartment hallway. He said, "That's your mother? She's so *heavy*." He was laughing, incredulous. He wasn't talking about her weight; she was short, thin, and pretty. It was the heaviness of her spirit, a darkness I could never put into words. A crushing weight that had burdened me from the time of my dad's death lifted a little. I had set myself the impossible task of making her happy, and nothing ever did.

John didn't let up about moving in. Eventually, we set a date. As the days ticked by, the date loomed like a neon sign I couldn't turn off, blocking out other thoughts.

Fifteen minutes before he was due to arrive, though, I panicked, jumped in my car, and drove towards New York on the Taconic Parkway. My thoughts raced. Why had I asked him to live with me? He probably wasn't coming. If he did come, he would leave. He would go back to his wife and children. How could I have been so stupid? He wasn't coming.

Although lost in thought, I spotted John in his orange Peugeot heading in the opposite direction on the parkway toward my house. I jerked up in my seat. I wondered if I should continue to New York City, where I had a good friend. She wouldn't mind if I needed a place to stay. I would take a break and get some perspective.

Instead, I slowed down. I pictured John banging on the locked door and an icy fury taking hold. I turned around at the next exit. When I pulled into the driveway behind him, he stepped out of his car.

"Did you just get here?" I asked brightly.

He looked at me, smoking. He made me wait, and then he said, "Where were you?"

I wanted to say, "I don't know," or "You pushed me into this." I was plunging off a cliff. I didn't want to be this person with feelings roiling around.

"I came back," I said, crying. "I'm glad you're here."

John had brought some clothes, a royal blue paella dish, a Julia Child cookbook, a Nikon camera, a couple of his drawings, skis, and a boat knife. I helped him carry it all upstairs, neither of us speaking. I lingered in the kitchen while John set his things down in the living room. We still hadn't spoken, but I was beginning to take in that he was there.

John was in such turmoil. He was miserable about leaving his daughter, Raegan, now nine, and his young son, Shae, three. Guilt colored our evenings as John drank himself to sleep, and I pictured myself as the adulterous other woman.

He said, "You may have hitched your wagon to the wrong star."

When we picked up the children on Sundays for the afternoon, I'd duck down in the car while John faced his wife. Sliding up to peek through the car window, I imagined the bitter words they exchanged at the front door. Once in the car, Raegan chattered about her week, singing her latest choral songs, while Shae tried to get a word in. We would visit John's parents, and I marveled at the difference between his mother and mine. His mother had a sense of humor and taught the children about the plants in her garden.

I was enamored of this man who prepared sophisticated French dishes and could intuit the precise moment when a béchamel sauce was ready. Although I knew little about hockey, I watched Rangers' games on TV with him in bed and lustily cheered. We lazed on pillows on the floor around an old ship's hatch we converted into a table in our living room, John's arm enfolding me as we listened to Bob Dylan and Leon Russell. I loved how he looked at and listened to me.

When we fought, usually after a few beers or glasses of

wine, John would slam down the stairs and the Peugeot disappeared in a spray of gravel. I huddled in bed crying, imagining that he'd never come back. It didn't take much to lead to a fight—John would be irritable or lost in thought, and I'd complain he wasn't paying attention to me or lash out about how long it was taking him to get over the separation. He'd roll back in during the night, climb in bed, and we melted gratefully into each other, forgetting about the fight until the next time. He never told me where he went, but I figured he found a bar somewhere.

After John moved in, I had a dream in which I was sitting in a crowded train station at night, on a bench with other passengers next to a broad, plate glass window that reflected the high arched ceilings and glittering glass chandeliers inside. The window overlooked a busy downtown thoroughfare. Waiting for my train, I was alert yet absorbed in the book I was reading. Suddenly, a giant bare foot crashed through the window, and a big laughing bearded man popped through.

Looking back, I can still feel the thunderous jolt of John entering my life, the swell of my heart when I heard his steps on the stairs to the apartment after work, the sure-footed steps of a sailor.

Chapter Three
Dad

The bowline is an exceptionally versatile knot. It is quick to tie…it doesn't slip, and it doesn't jam.

—*www.apparent-wind.com/knots/*

The bowline was John's favorite knot. At first, when I tried to make one, a light tug would unravel it. When John made a bowline, the knot held. John insisted that I learn the bowline before we left on *Laughing Goat*. I practiced on the handle of a pail we kept in the cockpit locker until I could do it without thinking, and it would hold.

My dad would not have known a bowline from a half hitch, but like John's bowline, he held onto me even after he was gone.

My dad was the center of my universe. I would make up jokes to crack him up and write poems addressed to "Lou Cole on the Porch." I would watch him dunk coffee cake in his coffee at breakfast and close his eyes as he took a sweet, soppy bite. On Saturday mornings, he brought me to his office downtown and lunch at Howard Johnson's while my mother attended garden club meetings. We ate ice cream and wrote notes to each other on the napkins.

One time, when I was around nine, he wrote, "I liked your story this week about the planets. How is your newspaper going?"

I had started the *Morley Road News* with a friend across the street. I wrote it, and she was supposed to make copies and coerce her younger brother into delivering it, though I was never sure if she did.

"Mrs. Hickenshniffer goes shopping for her family's trip to Mars this week." I jotted down the note, referring to my serial about Mrs. Hickenshniffer and her thirteen children.

I jumped in my seat in anticipation as he wrote me back. I watched his hand, the graceful fingers holding the fountain pen, the small hairs glowing in the sunlight, and the dark red stone gleaming on his gold ring. He looked gentle and smart, like a professor. I pounced on the napkin before he slid it over. "Keep it up!" he wrote.

My favorite picture of us was taken in a photo booth at Woolworth's five-and-dime store in our winter coats. Our glasses glinted companionably, matching our nerdy smiles. We looked like a couple of book lovers anticipating an afternoon of browsing through a bookstore. I imagine him waiting until just before the flash and saying, "Susie, keep your eyes open."

We traded knock-knock jokes, and Dad challenged me to spell silly words like pickle. He tried to win me over to Adlai Stevenson, who ran for president against General Eisenhower in 1952, and whom my dad considered a great man. I responded by marching around chanting, "I like Ike!" On country drives, he would roll down his window and moo at the cows, to my delight. On summer nights, even if he were reading, he would take the time to examine the fireflies I caught.

He was fifty-six when he died of heart disease. I was ten.

Even now, saying that my father died is hard. Losing him was like falling off the edge of a cliff, a free fall with no hospitable landing. The center of gravity that had held me up, though I hadn't noticed how central it was, had vanished. I could not make sense of it.

A boy in my grade lost his dad around the same time. I didn't want anything to do with that boy...he looked as sad as I felt. He was in the other fifth-grade class, so I hardly saw him at school. He blushed when anyone talked to him.

He lived on the next street over from mine, and one Sunday, I was practicing jacks on the sidewalk when I spotted him walking with his mother. He glanced at me. I glared back, afraid that he would burst into tears and blubber about his dad. I was relieved when he clasped his mother's hand, and they turned for home. I did not understand then that despite my valiant effort, I could not erase the pain of losing my dad.

After Dad died, my brother moved back home to help my mother run my dad's steel brokerage. My brother had been in the Navy after flunking out of Cornell. My dad's office had been a wonderland of typewriters, adding machines, drawing paper, and pencils. Now, it echoed with the shouts of my paranoid mother and brother, who screamed at each other all day from adjoining desks about mistakes they made. Neither had any business experience. Over dinner, they criticized each other, railed against enemies like the government, and spewed forth loony money-making ideas, "million-dollar" gadgets that never went anywhere. Some nights, we watched home movies. I loved seeing my dad on screen and hearing him talk, but the emptiness of the room after the lights came on made me so nauseous, I would go straight to bed.

I struggled through my teens, locked in anger at my dad because he had left and furious with my mother, who traveled frequently on cruises looking for a new husband, leaving me alone with my brother, who brought women home. I would lock myself in my bedroom to avoid him, but sometimes, as I listened from behind the door, I heard screams, and at least once, a girl ran out of the house sobbing. I did not feel safe. My brother was less of a threat when my mother was home, but she did little to help me, a young girl lost in grief.

In this post-Dad world, the family myths that had loosely formed during his lifetime—I was smart, my sister was promiscuous, and my brother, mentally disturbed— grew like tumors. I hung out with my brainy best friend and earned As but had little fun. My sister had flagrant affairs, and my brother became unhinged. When I was fifteen, he was jailed for rape. Though I was glad he was out of the house, my mother was even more preoccupied than usual until she bribed a judge to release him.

Although my grades slipped when my brother was in jail, my test scores made up for it, and I got into Barnard in New York City. My best friend would go to Radcliffe. We were eager to leave Cleveland behind. My dad would have beamed with pride that I made it into the Ivy League.

New York led me to John. Still, my past lingered. When John would leave on a business trip, I would shake with sobs and give myself over to feelings of utter abandonment. I didn't do so deliberately, but with each departure, I relived my dad's death. I was convinced I would never see John again.

One day after John and I had lived together for a few months in Croton-on-Hudson, as I sorted through a box of old family photos, a yellowed napkin fluttered out with a faded orange and turquoise Howard Johnson's logo, marked with my dad's elegant script and my uphill scrawl. As sunlight slanted across the wood floor, I hugged myself and sobbed—wracking, heaving sobs—and allowed myself to remember how much I loved my dad.

Chapter Four
XL

When John discovered a live-aboard community of boaters in Sausalito, California, on a business trip, he wanted to buy a boat to live on. Our first boat, *XL*, was an original 1903 Fire Island ferryboat, forty-eight feet long. *XL* had carried passengers from Bay Shore, Long Island, to Fire Island.

John spotted *XL* in a New York Times classified ad. We bought her from Woody, who lived on the boat with his wife and baby at Oyster Bay Yacht Club and held up his jeans with a rope. *XL's* hull sparkled with a fresh coat of white paint. The spacious, sunny interior had a Franklin stove for heat and comfortable wicker chairs. Stairs led to an upper deck with sun lounges.

When the boatyard hauled *XL* out of the water for inspection, stinky masses of seaweed and mud, along with thousands of snail-like barnacles, clung to nearly every inch of the bottom.

"You got a real garden under there," said one of the workers, as the others grunted in agreement.

The surveyor, a crusty New Englander, tapped a small hammer in different spots. He said, "This hull will outlive you."

We were pleased that he felt the boat would hold together. Only later did we learn that his nickname was Blind George.

As we worked on *XL* nights and weekends that first summer, other boaters would stop by to offer encouraging remarks like, "You know the two best days in a boat owner's life? The day you buy her and the day you sell her." Gleefully, they would spell out the toil and expense to repair an old wooden boat.

Although John had helped on his dad's sailboat, we had a lot to learn. John taught me to operate a palm sander, choose the right grit of sandpaper, roll bottom paint, dig out the rot and mix two-part epoxy. Each evening we went home to the apartment exhausted.

While I showered off the grime, though, far from feeling daunted, I admired the jaunty curve of *XL*'s bow. I was at ease among rumbling travel-lifts, riggers shouting from atop masts, sanders blasting, and fishy low tide smells. The boatyard evoked a memory of the flats in downtown Cleveland where my dad worked in the steel business amid tall stacks spewing fiery exhaust and men loading trucks with steel beams.

After John and I finished painting and repairing *XL's* bottom, we left the boatyard in Connecticut to head to Mamaroneck, New York, where we had arranged for a mooring. It was my first time on the water.

John, who had never run a large boat before, backed *XL* out of the slip. The steering wheel was in the sleeping cabin, which overlooked the bow. Sweat dripped from his forehead as he worked the levers. His eyes narrowed to anguished slits.

"The throttle's stuck."

I wasn't sure what a throttle was and ran in circles in the small open enclosure at the bow, shouting, "What is it?

What's going on?"

As *XL* sped forward toward a small knot of people waving goodbye on the dock, they split in all directions. I ducked inside. We crashed into a small fishing boat, but miraculously, the boat wasn't scratched.

John said, "We've got to get out of here." I nodded, unable to speak.

John tinkered with the throttle, and *XL* edged away from the dock. We didn't look back. Once out on the Sound, far from any other boats, John put the boat in neutral, and we climbed the stairs to the top deck. Lying back on lounge chairs, we gazed down the Sound from the majestic height of our upper deck and could hardly believe that this bright, airy ferryboat was our new home.

On the way back down into the cabin, John slipped on the stairs and landed on the engine. We had left the cover off in case it overheated. Bloody welts and burns slashed across his back. I grabbed rags to stanch the blood. Our outdated first aid kit was useless, but we did have acetaminophen.

Every time a wave hit, the bed rolled to the other side of the sleeping cabin, and wicker furniture slid around the main salon. None of the furniture was built-in, as it was on most boats. My job was to ensure John had enough cold beer while he steered.

John asked me to check on the dinghy that we towed from the stern. A bulkhead blocked his view. I leaned into the hallway and peered towards the rear where there should have been a back wall. Instead, a vista opened of the water and shoreline. The dinghy was bouncing along in the water behind us. I told him the dinghy was fine, but something was wrong. He raced back and rabidly eyed the water.

"The transom fell off."

The transom, a twelve-foot long, two-inch thick wall on the stern that normally enclosed the bottom half of the boat, had vanished. John spotted it floating beside us, *"XL, New York"* emblazoned across the middle. He hurled a rope overboard to lasso it and missed. Then, he dove over the side, yelling over his shoulder, "You'll have to turn on a dime!"

I was now alone on a forty-eight-foot ferryboat. Before the trip on *XL*, I hadn't been on any boat larger than a rowboat, yet John expected me to steer. I clutched the wheel, and my feet froze to the spot. How did I get myself into this? What if I couldn't find John? Lightheaded, I tried to get my bearings. I didn't see him.

John learned to swim when his mother made him jump off the dock in Greenwich into Long Island Sound. He learned to ski by strapping on skis and hurtling down the hill. I had grown up without any aspirations toward physical bravery. I longed to hide under a blanket until the situation went away, and I seethed with resentment that John had put me here.

XL staggered on. Sun sparkled off the ripples racing across the Sound. The bright blue sky stretched out, and each wavelet that brushed across the green-gray water cracked like a whip against the hull. A pale blob caught my eye in the water to my left, breaking up the ripples. It resolved into John, swimming for the boat.

I exhaled and choked out a laugh as he towed the massive hunk of wood. I pulled a lever, hoping the boat would slow down. For a moment, I felt like a ship's captain in charge of a daring rescue. John got close enough to hoist himself up and reached into the cooler for a beer. I cried with relief.

He was soaked and bruised, his back covered in bright red scrapes from his earlier fall. He drank the beer and steered. I found more acetaminophen.

Dusk was falling as we limped into Mamaroneck Harbor. I stood on the bow with a boathook ready to swoop for the mooring, but when we found it, we were going too fast to pick it up. Just as I thought it was hopeless, we hit a nearby boat, caromed backward, and I hooked the mooring. John shut off the engine, and the boat stopped moving. We went to bed and fell asleep instantly.

The next morning as the sky lightened, I woke up. *XL* was pointing in a different direction than when we went to bed.

"John, wake up." I shook him.

"What?"

"The boat moved. We're not in the same place as when we went to sleep."

He looked out the window. "It's the tide change." He turned over and fell back asleep. We were affected by the tide change? Until then, I knew about tides only through literary allusions.

In the early morning, I was up at first light and watched the sky lighten to yellow and pink as the sun rose from the horizon. We cleaned up the boat and puttered around in our dinghy. John examined the errant transom, which had served as an entrance ramp when the ferryboat was in service, and found the culprit, tiny eyehooks not strong enough to hold. We would purchase heftier fastenings.

We debated checking on the fishing boat that we had crashed into in Norwalk, but imagining the wrath of a sinewy fisherman and his angry relatives, we decided not to. A marine policeman inspected the boat we hit in Mamaroneck, which appeared undamaged. When he asked for our boat papers, we were shocked that bureaucracy could ensnare us even on the water. Neither of us had paid taxes for several years, and we each had piles of unpaid traffic tickets. We hoped to stay under the radar and not hear from the police again.

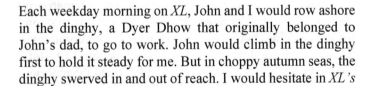

Each weekday morning on *XL*, John and I would row ashore in the dinghy, a Dyer Dhow that originally belonged to John's dad, to go to work. John would climb in the dinghy first to hold it steady for me. But in choppy autumn seas, the dinghy swerved in and out of reach. I would hesitate in *XL*'s doorway before jumping, as John hooted with laughter.

The Dyer Dhow is a nine-foot fiberglass boat with

wooden gunwales, seats, and mast. Originally built in Rhode Island of plywood in the early 1940s, the Dyer Dhow was a rescue boat for the Pacific front in World War II. Our little boat had seen better days. The gunwale was splintered, the centerboard leaked, and we had removed the mast and seats for repair. It was a sailing dinghy, but we had yet to sail her.

Perched on a pile of old lifejackets, John rowed while I bailed water sloshing over the bow with a coffee can. When I rowed, John would yell, "Pull! Pull! Starboard! Starboard!" I understood the urgency and pulled with all my strength, though I didn't fully grasp that the force of my rowing could keep us from capsizing.

When we reached shore, we would race into the bushes to change into our business clothes, which we stored in garbage bags in our cars. If one of us forgot a car key, we had to return to the boat and repeat the trip. On those days, we usually called in sick.

XL had no electricity. We used hurricane lamps and flashlights. We bathed in a tub the size of a double sink. As autumn wore on, we huddled in sweaters under a warm blanket in front of the Franklin stove. I read *Living on the Earth* and wrapped lettuce in damp paper towels to stay fresh. John read *Wooden Boat* magazines and learned about boat repairs. He was our carpenter. I was the boat's plumber.

XL's head had an unusually long waste hose winding through the bilge, a damp smelly no-man's land between the floor and the bottom of the hull. The hose was frequently clogged. To repair it, I squeezed into the bilge, lay on my back, undid the clamps, and shoved a plumbing snake through the hose.

"Pump!" I yelled through the floorboards to John.

John would convulse with laughter at the image of me stuck in the bilge, wrestling with the stinky waste hose. I had grown up expecting boys to hold doors open for me. I had never repaired anything before, but John made it clear that we were in this together, and I had to do my part.

I held my breath and scrabbled out of the way in case a

foul mess shot out of the end. When done, I screwed in the clamp and climbed out, trying not to throw up. A friend bought me a "Headhunter" t-shirt with two crossed plungers.

Potted red geraniums flourished in the bright sunlight that poured into the main cabin. I set up an easel in a corner, painted large canvases with clouds of light colors, and propped them against the walls. We rowed home after work under pink and orange skies at sunset.

When winter came, we moved to a marina in Stamford, Connecticut, for the luxuries of electricity on the dock and heated restrooms with showers. We met a motley crew of others living aboard their boats: divorcees, drifters, drug users, and dreamers saving money to sail away.

We all slipped and slid down icy ramps, arms full of groceries or boat supplies that at any moment could tumble into the water. To fill our water tanks, we dragged long heavy hoses from the marina office down to our boats and back up again. The live-aboard boaters got so sick of fighting off water rats that we impaled one of our kills on the dock manager's door to compel the boatyard to exterminate.

As primitive as the living conditions were, though, I loved the hushed harbor in winter where water splashed past snowy banks onshore. Shrieking seagulls swooped high overhead to drop clams on the docks with enough force to smash them open to eat. Bluish light sifted through the hatch during the day. At night, steaks from the butcher shop sizzled on the stove or, if we made it to the fish market in time, clams boiled in a fragrant mix of wine and herbs. The harbor boasted large affluent homes, but I wouldn't have traded places with any of them.

John's parents lived across town, and we would drop in at their house to do laundry and shower. John argued with his dad in a way that I never dared with my mother. His dad would criticize John's treatment of his ex-wife and did not understand John's career path. John had left the market research company where we had worked and taken a job at the boatyard. He had new friends like Shaky Jake, the ironworker who fell off a ladder and broke his shoulder. John didn't intend to stay at the boatyard but hadn't yet figured out his next move. John's boatyard stories did not amuse his dad, a partner in an engineering firm.

After some months, John interviewed with a management recruiter, who suggested jobs in New York. John balked at joining the grim commuter masses in gray flannel suits, like his dad. But he was drawn to New York's energy, and the idea of working in an advertising agency intrigued him.

John purchased new clothes for job interviews. The day of his first interview, he appeared on deck in a spiffy white suit and Panama hat. His new boatyard friends catcalled and whistled as John made his way down the dock.

John landed a job in market research at J. Walter Thompson, at the time the largest ad agency in New York. He wore a suit that he hung on the back of his office door to client meetings but otherwise wore jeans and topsiders—no socks—when his colleagues wore suits and ties. At the office, he became known as the "thinker." Some mornings, John didn't make it to work when we had water up to the floorboards, and we had to pump the boat out before she sank.

John's mother would stop by the boat with fresh tomatoes and flowers from her garden. If we were not home, she left a basket for us on the dock outside the door. John adored his mother, and she thought he was the funniest human being on the planet. His dad had traveled a lot for work when John was young, and though John respected him, he never formed a strong bond with him. His mother begged John to make up with his dad.

John's relationship with his parents fascinated me. In my family, so much was unspoken. John's family expressed how they felt.

When John and I took *XL* out on the water, calamity would befall us. The steering would fail, and we would drift helplessly, or the engine would blow coils of thick black smoke that curled past the white curtains out of the windows. As his captain's hat, John wore a five-legged red jester's cap with bells on the ends. Somehow, he always got us back to shore. He would pump his arm in victory and proclaim, "Cheated death again."

After we had lived aboard for about four years, we hauled *XL* out of the water for repairs. *XL's* leaks had multiplied to the point where John was sleeping with one foot on the floor. In the heat of summer, we spent weekends and nights repeating the work we had done when we first bought the boat: digging out worn caulking, stiffening the rotten wood with epoxy, sanding and painting the topsides and bottom.

We stayed with John's parents for a few weeks while the boat was out of the water. I imagined that they thought of me as the other woman, and I kept out of their way. But when I was sick with flu, his mother proffered cool washcloths and acetaminophen. On nights John had to work late, they cracked jokes about him that made me laugh.

After a last backbreaking push in the early fall of 1976, we asked the boatyard to launch the boat.

The next morning as John and I entered the gate, a fireman yelled, "Get back!"

A fire truck and a cluster of firemen hovered near the water. We raced over.

The tip of a black smokestack stuck out of the water, pointing sideways like a broken finger. Through the murky water of the Norwalk River in Connecticut, I could make out a milky white shape. *XL* looked like a stricken animal, her soft white skin undulating helplessly under the yellowish-brown water. Red smudges, the remains of my scarlet geraniums, floated down the river.

XL was on her side. A pump had shorted out during the night, and she had filled with water and sunk. The firemen told us not to look, but we kept vigil while they raised her.

As we stepped inside that afternoon, our deck shoes slid on the brown slime that coated the floorboards, along with the orange Scandinavian dining table that had been our first big purchase together, and the stacks of Beatles and Bob Dylan records. The stench was overpowering, a blend of sea muck and dead fish. I held onto the doorframe to keep from slipping, frozen in place, unable to move or think.

John blamed himself for not staying aboard the boat, but if he had, he might have gone down with it. John insisted on remaining on board that night, and I went to his parents' house for blankets.

I drove like a maniac. Glassy-eyed with shock, I ran into the kitchen where John's mother and Pat, John's sister who lived nearby, dropped what they were doing.

"The boat sank!" I stood there in disbelief while my words hung in the air. Yesterday, at the relaunch, John's parents had brought a bottle of champagne.

"What can we do? What do you need?" his mother asked.

Pat and I raced to the linen closet for sheets and blankets, and John's mother put together food and drinks.

Over the next week, with friends' help, we scrubbed *XL* down with bleach, soap, and vinegar and threw out whatever couldn't be salvaged. Having lost so much, John asked his parents for financial help to get back on our feet and suggested that I ask my mother, too. When I dismissed the idea, he said, "This is what families do. They help each other."

My mother was a survivor, albeit a paranoid one. Everyone was out to cheat her, even her children. Not only did I never ask for help, but I also waved my independence like a flag of honor. But John had a point. I strode to the paint-spattered phone booth in the boatyard, dialed her number, and when she picked up, told her our boat had sunk, and we had lost everything. An aching lump formed in my throat, admitting such a setback to my mother, to whom I rarely confided what transpired in my life.

Like many people, she never grasped why we would want to live on a boat in the first place instead of a nice suburban house. Calmly, she asked where we would live.

"Will you move in with John's parents in Greenwich?"

His parents lived in Stamford now, but while John was growing up, had lived in Greenwich, which my mother correctly associated with "old money" and wealth. John's parents, however, fell in the income mid-range in Greenwich. She imagined us living in a mansion with a staff of servants. Her false assumptions infuriated me. I pictured her self-satisfied smirk.

"No," I screamed, "we're fixing up the boat and will move back in. We need your help."

"What about John's parents? Why can't they help?"

"They *are* helping," I shouted. I was crying now. His parents had not questioned us, even though John and his dad were at odds.

"You bitch!" I shouted, hardly believing my voice. I had never shouted at her. I slammed the phone down.

Shaking, I ran to the boat. As my crying subsided, I told John about the call. Years of unexpressed anger at my mother now rained down on John for suggesting I call her. John thought I should call her back since I hadn't allowed her to answer.

"Are you crazy? I never want to speak to her again. I knew she would do this. How could you have thought it was a good idea? I knew it."

I attacked *XL's* floor with a boat brush. But the call forced me, at least at that moment, to face a reality about my mother that I preferred to gloss over: she was not there for me.

We finished cleaning up the boat and moved back aboard but did not feel the same about *XL* after the sinking. Before, even when we woke up with water rising through the floorboards, we had faith that we could keep *XL* afloat. Now, that faith was broken. Within a few months, we sold *XL* to a hang-glider enthusiast who wanted to park her somewhere and smoke weed with friends using his extensive bong collection.

Chapter Five
Phaedrus

Our next boat was a fifty-ton, fifty-foot Colin Archer-designed ketch built in Norway in the 1920s for the North Sea. The hull was double-ended like a canoe. A gleaming wood pilothouse dominated the deck. We had admired the pleasing lines and polished wood from afar at the marina where we lived aboard *XL*.

The owner of the Norwegian ketch invited us to look at the boat. He lounged on the main cabin settee where I was already picturing myself and told us that the boat was originally built to ferry boat pilots out of North Sea harbors to guide big ships in. As sea stories stretched on in the golden afternoon light, I imagined hearty Norwegian captains guzzling grog at the dining table and steeling themselves for the transfer to a ship. The pilots jumped in freezing water, and as their beards stiffened with ice, sailors from the ship hauled them aboard.

The main cabin had floor-to-ceiling wainscoting that

curved around to form the back wall of a deep settee. A large overhead hatch let in lots of light. The interior was a rough-hewn oak version of our future boat, *Laughing Goat*. John and I would sleep in the roomy aft cabin behind the pilothouse.

Everything was out-sized: the heavy boom, thick Dacron sails, eight-foot-long bowsprit, three-inch-thick hull, and nine-foot draft. The owner casually mentioned that he never took the boat out. We attributed his timidity to cowardice and plunked down a deposit. We named her *Phaedrus* after a character in a book we were reading, *Zen and the Art of Motorcycle Maintenance*. Phaedrus was the main character's alter ego on a quest to find a higher quality of life, a quest that eventually drove him insane.

John finally had a sailboat. However, *Phaedrus* was too heavy to tack under sail. Tacking across the wind is the only way to sail if the wind is against you—sailing at an angle to the wind, zigzagging to move forward. Each time we took her out, John tried to nudge *Phaedrus* closer to the wind. He attempted different sail combinations and trims. But *Phaedrus*, a pilot-boat, wasn't designed for close-hauled sailing. We were constantly "in irons"—wallowing, sails flopping, going nowhere as we struggled to bring the boat around to the other side of the wind.

The engine, built for North Sea conditions, had a reverse pitch prop. John rotated a heavy wheel located to the right of the steering wheel thirteen times to go from forward to reverse. Not only did he have to keep count, but steering from inside the pilothouse, he couldn't see over the high bow and relied on me to judge distances.

Docking the boat resembled a Chinese fire drill. It was my job to direct John when to slow down or turn. Rarely did I give him decent directions for a smooth landing. Most often, we crashed into the dock; I hopped out and tied us up while John declared his usual, "Cheated death again."

We now understood all too well the former owner's reluctance to take the boat out. John's nickname became

Captain Crash.

Our first year living on the boat, 1978, we got married in Stamford Harbor. We had been living together for six years. Although a friend, Anne, and I had plotted to persuade our boyfriends to marry us, I didn't hear John when he asked me, and he had to ask again.

I wonder now, looking back, how I could not have heard him. I was marrying a man who smoked three packs a day, drank heavily, thumbed his nose at authority, and was happiest at sea. None of that bothered me, but the depth of my feeling for him terrified me.

I spent the day before the wedding crouched in a corner of Anne's apartment while she cut and glued large paper flowers—blue, yellow, green, lavender, scarlet—and wove them onto long strings, which we tied to the rigging and raised to the top of the mast. I babbled about how I wanted to have a child, but John did not. Maybe he would never change his mind. Maybe I shouldn't get married. I hadn't invited my family to the wedding. What was I getting myself into?

Anne, who was still waiting for her longtime boyfriend to propose, kept asking me if I loved him. The answer was always yes.

"Then just take this step and see what happens," she said.

John and I stood at the bow for the sunset ceremony in Stamford Harbor. Paper flowers fluttered from the rigging. My wedding dress consisted of a long glowing silk scarf and skirt in a rich burgundy from Norma Kamali's shop in New York. I draped the scarf artfully on top and pinned yellow flowers in my hair. John wore a red-white-and-blue madras sports jacket and jeans. The sky glowed pale pink at the horizon. We were barefoot.

We had forty guests. Raegan, fifteen, had her first glass of champagne, and Shae, nine, was the ring-bearer. A friend ferried guests, including the minister, from the dock in a borrowed Boston Whaler.

The next morning, we embarked for a honeymoon on Block Island. Out on the Sound, I jumped up on the roof of the pilothouse, dancing and waving my wedding band. When *Phaedrus* entered Great Salt Pond Harbor in Block Island adorned with flowers, fishing boats hailed us to ask if we were the blessing of the fleet.

I got laid off from the market research job in Croton-on-Hudson. Like John when he first interviewed in New York, I had little idea of the working world beyond the small companies that had employed me. In multi-colored flowing pants and blouse, which struck me as a businesslike upgrade from the jeans I usually wore, I interviewed with a management recruiter. The recruiter thought I was wearing lounging pajamas.

Nevertheless, a large market research firm hired me. My background was in qualitative research—small-sample in-depth research of customers' needs and motivations. The firm specialized in large-scale quantitative studies, and I would head up a new qualitative effort.

I was a round peg in a square hole. No one knew what to do with me. I argued with my boss, the owner of the firm. I knew more than he did about qualitative research but a lot less about running a business or getting along with colleagues. Imagining myself to be indispensable, I was stunned when he fired me.

I started my own business. My office was on the boat, and I named the business Phaedrus, Inc. I listed potential clients, including John's colleagues to whom he had recommended me. I stared at the phone, brewed coffee, paced, and stared again. I had never asked anyone for business and wondered why these people would hire me. Eventually, after many aborted dialing attempts, I would remind myself that if I didn't do anything, nothing would happen. I snatched up the phone and dialed quickly before I could change my mind. My sales call rate was two or three a day.

One of my first clients was Jaguar sports cars. I interviewed Jaguar owners around the country about the Jaguar XJ-S, a new sports model. I was so nervous about presenting the results to the client in New York that as I wrote the presentation, I convinced myself I would never actually leave the boat.

On the day of the presentation, portfolio case in hand, grim but determined, I took the train into New York and arrived at Jaguar's advertising agency. I stacked up my storyboards on an easel, my heart pounding, while people in the room chattered. John had advised me that after finishing each board, I casually toss it on the ground. When I sent the first storyboard flying, my panic subsided. As John predicted, I loosened up and had fun as I had when I interviewed Jaguar owners for the study.

We lived aboard *Phaedrus* for ten years. When we got together with friends on other boats, the conversation centered on sailing away. We all imagined sailing through the Panama Canal and across the Pacific someday.

In reality, we had old wooden boats in need of care. One friend became so adept with epoxy he replaced all the planking on one side of his hull and helped us replace a plank on ours. Frayed blue tarps covered boatbuilding materials on the dock. On weekends, we would sand, scrape, and repair rot while sailors in shiny new boats sped past with comments like, "Must be a labor of love."

It became harder to find marinas that would accept live-aboard boaters. Though our boats were more-or-less seaworthy, the marinas and wealthy homeowners in the area considered them eyesores. One by one, the live-aboard boaters peeled off, selling their boats, and moving on land. Although by this time, John and I knew that *Phaedrus* was not the boat we would sail off on, John viewed moving on land as a betrayal of the dream.

We made a fateful decision to spiff up our boat instead. The classic sailboats we fantasized about had teak decks—

long clean ribbons of curving hardwood. Although we couldn't afford teak, we ripped off the old marine burlap that protected *Phaedrus'* deck and hired the boatyard to sand and caulk the fir planks underneath. After several weeks and great expense, strips of rosy, like-new yellow-brown fir soared up the deck from stern to bow.

But at the first rain, the deck leaked like a sieve. The burlap we hated had kept the rain out. Now, the cushions in the main cabin and our good clothes got soaked as we ducked drips and positioned pails strategically to catch leaks.

We demanded that the boatyard fix it. They tried but failed. We refused to pay for the work beyond the initial deposit. Eventually, we left and went to a different marina. Although we tried, we never did eradicate all the leaks.

One rainy day, I peeked into the hanging locker to see dark wet blotches marring a soft red wool skirt that I had bought on a trip to Paris. I waved the skirt in John's face.

"I want to buy a house. I can't take this anymore!"

To my surprise, John agreed.

Chapter Six
Brookside Drive, Kate, and Laughing Goat

We moved into 425 Brookside Drive, a dark red farmhouse on a hill in Fairfield, Connecticut. The Mill River, a narrow, bubbling stream shaded by oaks and wild bushes, burbled along the edge of the property. A trail of wide flat stones curved through the trees down to the front door as though leading to Hansel and Gretel's cottage. After fifteen years of living on the water, I had a home on land.

The first night in the house, we hung around the kitchen, putting together sandwiches for dinner. We leaned on each other as we walked from the kitchen through the still-bare living room into the den, carrying our plates. Unused to all the space, we thought the house was enormous. We slumped onto the love seat and watched TV. When John had to go to the bathroom, he made his way to the back deck and urinated over the side, just as he had off the bows of the boats on which we had lived.

My desire for a child ratcheted up. In my twenties, I had been horrified when I visited a friend from college who was stuck at home with a sick little boy, diarrhea running down his legs, and was glad I wasn't in her shoes. In my thirties, though, my feelings changed.

But having the desire and accepting it were poles apart. I knew that John did not want more children. I loved John's children and hoped maybe that would be enough. I didn't like a conflict with John or anyone. I pointed out to myself that I had won John's agreement to move off the boat, a victory.

When I was nearly forty, John's son Shae, fifteen, came to live with us. He was having trouble with his stepfather and not doing well at school. Tall and lanky, with long, light brown hair, usually topped with a black beret, he carried a sketchpad filled with a dark graphic novel that he occasionally, sullenly shared with us.

Thoughts of having a child would descend upon me at night as I lay next to John. I tried to talk myself out of it, imagining John's objections and berating myself. We had enough to deal with, trying to get Shae through school. John had been clear that he hadn't wanted more children. Couldn't I content myself with what we had?

Eventually, Shae left school. He alternated between lounging upstairs reading comics while I worked in my office one floor below and ground my teeth, a new habit, or disappearing for days. Over the years, John had writhed in agony as his ex-wife—in John's estimation—coddled Shae. John was determined to teach Shae how to get along in the world and instill an expectation of consequences for his behavior. It didn't help John's cause that after a few drinks, his frustration with Shae escalated, and he would lose his temper.

After a few weeks of Shae's lounging-and-disappearing routine, John gave him a three-month deadline to find another place to live. Shae continued lounging, as John repeatedly warned him that he was going to enforce the deadline. In desperation, I called my nephew in Boston who offered Shae a job painting his house. After Shae left for

Boston, although we were relieved, we both felt guilty.

Over dinners, John would say, "I wish I could have done better with Shae."

John's misery about Shae pricked at me during my convoluted late-night conversations with myself. The timing was terrible to bring up having another child with John, but on the other hand, the timing was never good. Was this my opening? One night, I said, "I'm not going to use contraception. At my age, I don't think anything will happen, anyway."

I said it while my heart pounded. I was amazed I had gotten it out. I could hardly continue cutting the meat and lifting the fork.

John didn't respond. I looked over to make sure he was listening. Measured against the force of his unyielding stance in the past, his silence was an opening into which my heart leaped.

In the spring of 1988, I missed a period. After the doctor's office confirmed that I was indeed pregnant, I hung up the phone and sat on the edge of my bed. The quickening in my stomach fluttered through my body. I pictured myself strolling down Brookside Drive with my baby to the duck pond at the end of the street. Doubts about how to raise a child rose. I would have to read about it. I abandoned the idea of working any more that day and thought about how I would tell John.

I picked him up at the station that night. When he got in the car, a pang of guilt shot through me. I was about to deliver a zinger to someone I loved. I waited until John was partway through his first Mount-Gay-and-tonic.

"I have some news." He looked away from the TV screen, where Robin McNeil was talking about President Raegan.

"I'm pregnant." He stared at me, taking a sip of his drink. I thought of saying more—about how, as much as I wanted a baby, I wasn't sure myself how I felt, that I hadn't imagined I'd get pregnant so quickly, that my business had been taking off, and I didn't know what this would mean. We looked at each other.

"Okay," he said. I released my breath into the silence.

"This doesn't change anything," he said. "We're going cruising. I know you. You'll get all settled in with the baby. I'm not commuting into New York until I'm seventy, and I keel over from a heart attack on the train. You can come or not, but I'm going sailing."

"I'll come," I said, thinking of the new baby. We didn't have a boat yet for long-distance cruising. There was still plenty of time. I wouldn't have to deal with it now, and maybe John would change his mind.

The months flew by. One night the week before Thanksgiving, eight months pregnant, I picked John up as usual from the Fairfield train station. His resolute expression stopped me from launching into a litany of complaints about how fat and uncomfortable I was.

He slid into the car and said, "That fucking dipshit P."

P. was John's new boss, who routinely took credit for John's ideas. John fantasized often about P.'s body whooshing past his window to an ignominious end on a pavement thirty floors below. That day, John had given a presentation during which his hands shook and his face was red. He had been drinking with colleagues the night before. The client wanted him off the account. P. offered John a thirty-day rehab program in Greenwich Hospital, paid for by the agency. John had to stop drinking, or he was out of a job.

Before I met John, I knew little about wines other than Manischewitz, but I now enjoyed long lunches sipping Pouilly Fuissé on John's expense account in Manhattan and lazy weekend afternoons at our favorite bars in Connecticut—snow falling outside, fire crackling in a corner fireplace, bottles gleaming like jewels against dark wood shelves. John, and now I, moved in a milieu where liquor flowed freely.

Drinking was fun. However, when we were first together, I had noticed that John would become morose as he drank, mired in guilt over leaving his children, and sometimes, when we were out sailing, I worried about his judgment if he had drunk too much. Those worries hadn't risen to a level where they bothered me, though.

John reluctantly decided to go to rehab. He would start the week after Thanksgiving.

John's sisters were elated. I was miserable. I was too fat to bend down and tie my shoes; the weather was gray, cold, and slushy, and I worried that the baby might come early while John was still in rehab. Family visits were only allowed on weekends, and I would miss him. Having a baby at forty-two felt like enough of a change in my life. Now I would have to get used to a new John who did not drink. My obstetrician allowed me a few glasses of wine a week, and I feared I might have to give those up, too.

On the first weekend of John's stay, I participated unenthusiastically in a counseling session with other spouses and relatives. The counselor asked about a typical day, and I described our Saturdays. John would chug a few cold beers in the morning and have a few drinks at lunch. After that, I would drive around to shop at the vegetable market, the fruit stand, and Shop Rite while John slept in the car. The other participants nodded sympathetically. The counselor used my story as an example of denial, which irked me.

On weekend visits, he was distant. The social workers at the hospital explained how hard it was to stay sober and encouraged patience for our relatives. However, I was about to have a baby and the thought of going through labor frightened me. I had no room for compassion for anyone else. I was waiting for John to finish his time "in the clink" and come home where I expected him to be patient and compassionate with *me*.

At home, he was irritable. He went back to work and concentrated on staying sober. I had little appreciation of how difficult a task that was. We had two more weeks until the due date, but Kate had other plans. At midnight on John's first Saturday home, water began dripping down my legs.

I stuck my head in the den where John was watching TV and squeaked, "I think my water broke. It's the first sign of labor." John laughed at my discomfiture. He hadn't laughed since he came home, and the sound briefly cheered me.

We went to bed, but stomach pains woke me. Anxiously panting, I poked John.

"What?" he asked groggily.

"I'm in labor. You have to wake up."

"How far apart are the contractions?" We had learned in Lamaze class that contractions increase in frequency and intensity as the baby nears delivery. My doctor had asked me to call her when they were six minutes apart.

"I don't know. You have to wake up and time them." I shook him. He turned over to go back to sleep.

"Time them yourself," he mumbled.

Taken aback, I grabbed John's watch and tried to focus. How could he be so mean? Was I supposed to start timing at the beginning of the contraction or the end? I lost track of the number of minutes. Eventually, I got out of bed and walked around. For the next few hours, I listened to Billie Holiday's albums while eating lemon Jell-O.

We went to the hospital at eleven o'clock the next morning. I was determined to have a natural childbirth. Two of our nieces, both of whom had children naturally, came to support me. John, who had just left a different wing of the hospital himself a few days ago, smoked outside and checked on me periodically.

The hours ticked by as I waddled up and down hospital corridors, a niece on each side, to stimulate enough cervical dilation to push the baby out. My doctor offered me an epidural, which I refused. She offered the epidural again and again. My nieces, who each had used midwives, held firm against the increasing pressure. However, I knew the doctor well. I had seen her for fifteen years and trusted her. Eventually, I asked to speak to John alone.

"What should I do? Maybe the doctor is right, but I've

always wanted a natural childbirth."

John said, "I don't know if this will help, but I'll share something I learned in rehab."

He recited the Serenity Prayer, which was new to me.

God grant me the serenity to accept the things I cannot change.

Courage to change the things I can.

And wisdom to know the difference.

Up to now, he had not talked about rehab. Looking into his eyes, I realized how tough the past month had been and how much John had accomplished. As we looked at each other, the divide between us melted. I wept. My conflict about whether to have the epidural evaporated, too. I told the doctor I wanted drugs.

The pain blessedly disappeared. Kate was born soon thereafter. Holding her in my arms for the first time, I drank in her perfect tiny features and her inquisitive stare and realized with a shock that she was a separate person with whom I would have to deal. Kate's first name was after John's mother and a feminist professor at Barnard I had admired; her middle name was after my dad.

When she cried, I would carry her back and forth through the living room, Kate on one arm and a child development book on the other as I flipped through pages to figure out what I should do. I worried about scarring her for life if I couldn't immediately soothe her. John dangled her upside down, plopped her on top of his head, and propped her on the couch against a Day-of-the-Dead skeleton we had bought in Mexico. He said, "She won't break."

After a few weeks, I began to trust my instincts. Home alone with Kate, I danced around the house with her in my arms, singing show tunes to her softly: "A Bushel and a Peck" and "I Could Have Danced All Night."

When Kate was about six months old, we sold *Phaedrus* to a shady character that made a small down payment and promised to pay the remainder over time; we never heard from him again. We bought a twenty-six-foot

Soling, a bright red racing boat originally designed for the Olympics, that we named *Red Dog*. For the first time, we owned a boat that didn't require a day of preparation before taking her out on the water.

Red Dog had no motor, and we would sail out of the harbor, tacking back and forth across the wind. Each time we tacked, the boom slammed over, the sails whipped furiously, and the sheets beat against the side of the boat. I tucked Kate under the overhang while I tended lines, and she cried at the noise.

Once we got out of the harbor into the Sound, the boat quieted, and I brought Kate back on my lap. She listened to the boat cutting through the water with a smile. John was delighted: Kate liked to sail.

The summer when Kate was one, John and I chartered a sailboat in Maine. We sailed into Southwest Harbor, home of the Hinckley boatyard. Hinckley sailboats were the gold standard. Whenever we spotted one on Long Island Sound, it would take our breaths away—classy, beautifully constructed, understated yet gorgeous. And well beyond our price range.

The entrance to Southwest Harbor is like a fjord, a narrow passage with high ground on either side. At sunset, we rounded the bend, the harbor opened, and about twenty Hinckley sailboats came into view, moored near the boatyard in the pale orange glow of dusk. The harbor was quiet except for seagulls cawing. John whistled.

"Will you look at that?"

Before that night, I would have sworn that Hinckley's boats were all constructed of wood, which, although we loved its natural beauty, required so much labor. But many of these graceful boats were fiberglass, and they were knockouts. Gaping, we imagined our next boat, *Laughing Goat*, into being.

Back home, sailing magazines piled up on John's side of the bed. He showed me photos of boats he especially liked and places he wanted to sail like the Rio Dulce, a remote river in Guatemala where Johnny Weissmuller had filmed the first Tarzan movie.

I volunteered at Kate's nursery school, helping children with projects, and reading to the class. I took Kate on playdates. Late in the afternoon, before picking up John at the train station, we watched cartoons in the den, Kate lying contentedly in my lap. I enjoyed having Kate's friends and cousins over and relished being Kate's mom. For a long time, I had worried that I was not fit for that role since my relationship with my mother was fraught and spiteful. I was afraid that I wouldn't know how to act otherwise.

In 1993, when Kate was four, we searched for an ocean-going sailboat. We flew to Fort Lauderdale, a boating mecca where glittering luxury yachts, heavy-duty racing sailboats, cigarette boats, and cruise ships sped past each other in the channel. At night, drawbridges clanged, and navigation lights twinkled in every direction.

A broker showed us a Bristol, a Peterson, a Cabo Rico, a Westsail, a New York 40, a CT, and others. We peered into chain lockers, admired intricate cabinetry, and checked out rigs and sails. The more boats we saw, the more certain we became about what we wanted: a classic design about forty-five feet long, an aft cabin that you could stand in, a spacious galley, a forward cabin for Kate, and a warm, homey feel.

A jolly, weathered older couple that had cruised in the Caribbean showed us a Peterson. The wife whipped out the water-maker, a device that turned salt water into drinking water. As she eagerly showed me how it worked, I thought about how little I knew of living on a boat in remote places where you needed to extract your drinking water from tubes.

In Florida, we stayed with friends who had lived on a sailboat across the dock from *XL*. They were excited about our new adventure. When my friend and I were doing dishes after dinner, she asked how I felt about buying a new boat and sailing off.

"It will be a while yet," I said.

I was still on a high from the past few days of our

window-shopping expedition. I imagined many such vacations in yachting centers around the country, seeking the perfect boat.

A couple of months after the Florida trip, John arranged to see a Mason 43 in Stamford harbor. Huddling together against the winter wind, we took in the smooth white hull, the thin gold stripe along the rub rail, the teak deck, and varnished rails. Quarter-rounds finished off each hatch. Where *Phaedrus* in her prime had workboat-type toughness, this boat brimmed with fine finish-work.

The broker forgot to leave the key. I knelt and peered through an aft cabin porthole. The teak deck, sheltered by the cabin top, felt warm through my jeans. Large berths hugged either side of the cabin. A wide hanging locker, gracefully arched with carved insets of contrasting woods, stood in between. A brass reading lamp perched above what I imagined as my side of the bed.

"A poor man's Hinckley," the broker called it, which set our hearts soaring. We had found the boat we wanted.

John sat down with me in the cockpit. As seagulls shrieked overhead, we remembered the winters on *XL* and *Phaedrus*. We had lived in the house in Fairfield about five years now, and as much as I loved it, I sometimes missed the wintry solitude of the docks. Our over-scheduled lives on land lacked the raw closeness to nature of living on the water.

We traipsed back toward the parking lot and stopped in at the bar overlooking the harbor. We buzzed with excitement under the blue lights of the bar. From a payphone, John called Ross, a friend who had lived across the dock from us and who had recently retired from General Foods to become a yacht broker. We asked him to find an older Mason 43 we could afford.

Within a few months, we flew down to Fort Lauderdale again to look at a 1982 Mason 43. We admired the elegant lines, crisp blue hull, and the myriad warm woods shining from each carefully constructed cabinet, rail, and bulkhead.

The owners had cruised for several years in the Caribbean. In a cabinet in the main salon, I found a handwritten letter the wife had written to a friend describing their adventures in the Virgin Islands. The pale blue notepaper smelled like a sun-washed beach.

Our offer was accepted. We hired a well-respected surveyor and requested a sea trial. We wanted to be sure the boat was seaworthy.

The day of the sea trial shone sunny, bright, and breezy. A hired captain steered the boat out of Fort Lauderdale's teeming harbor. John and I followed the surveyor around as he poked different spots with his hammer while the brokers chatted up forward. As we sailed out of the channel, the Atlantic Ocean spread before us. Our pale northern legs peeked out beneath our shorts. John and I looked at the blue horizon. Slightly woozy from a motion sickness pill, I imagined sailing for miles in soft, warm breezes.

Although she needed some repairs, the boat passed the survey with flying colors. We signed a contract. For the first time, we had a well-found boat capable of taking us past Long Island Sound to the far reaches of the ocean. I pushed away thoughts of what it would mean to leave home and head to sea. On the plane ride home, we were elated.

Myriad tasks unfurled into the future, from getting the boat documented and delivered up north, to making repairs, and purchasing equipment. John wanted to get everything right. I was glad John was so conscientious, and I imagined that it would take years to get ready. Maybe, I hoped, we would never even leave.

After a weekend brainstorming, we named her *Laughing Goat,* an amalgam of a famous racing boat, *Laughing Gull,* and the old goat whom John felt he was becoming.

Between attending my book club, volunteering at Kate's school, and holding a Seder over the Jewish holidays at my house, a tradition I suddenly resurrected from my childhood, I was laying brick after brick to cement my place in the community. If I could talk to myself then, I might gently say, "John wants this. He's been quietly steering toward it for years. This is going to happen. You and Kate are not staying here. You're going sailing."

Chapter Seven
Leaving Fairfield

John and I moored *Laughing Goat* in Milford, the town where his sister Pat and her husband Fred lived. We sailed on weekends in the summer and fall. Throughout the year, John steadily worked on the boat. Now that he was no longer drinking, he was amazed at his productivity in preparing the boat for a long sea voyage.

Following the surveyor's recommendations, John prioritized tasks, hiring help where needed. He wasn't afraid to throw himself into repairs in which he had no previous experience, like re-wiring the boat. Marine electricians were expensive and unavailable on remote islands. He read books and asked electricians for advice. We worried that our amateur efforts would electrocute us.

On the boat, I would scrunch into a locker to untangle the old wires as John raced to the electronic panel to turn on the circuit breaker.

"Ready?" he said.

"Yes," I grunted.

"Are you sure?"

"Yes!" I couldn't wait to get out of the stuffy, cramped locker.

"Sssssssssssst!" No matter how many times he did it, John's hiss startled me as he flipped the switch.

Despite John's progress on *Laughing Goat*, I envisioned my life centered in Fairfield for years to come. I gardened on weekends or helped John on the boat; we went out on date nights. I had a sitter for Kate, so I could work in my office downstairs. We took Kate and her best friend for Dairy Queen cones. Although my mother was still a crafty thorn in my side, and John and I had to travel on business more than I liked, my life rolled along smoothly.

We got a black-and-white female kitten, whom Kate named Itty Bitty. When we lived aboard *XL* and *Phaedrus*, John and I had a succession of outdoor cats to deter mice. Our favorite, a scrappy gray male on *Phaedrus*, chased dogs off the dock and perched on the mainsail when we sailed. He would hang on even as the boat tacked, and the boom swung over to the other side. Itty Bitty, though, had a tough time with a big white tomcat next door, which would maul her rear end. She still wanted to go outside, and John believed strongly that she should have freedom, but I felt sorry for her.

In first grade, Kate joined a soccer team. John and I cheered from the sidelines and passed out orange slices. Kate proved adept at digging in and coming up with the ball. I had not played sports as a child and swelled with pride when the coach would yell, "Way to hustle, Russell!" Russell was John and Kate's last name. In the feminist spirit of the 1970s, I kept my maiden name.

On date nights, John and I discussed sailing plans. We had not yet made a firm decision about when we were leaving or where we would go. When John brought it up, my worries swarmed.

"What about medical supplies? What will we do with

the house? How will we find kids for Kate to play with?" I asked.

One by one, John patiently swatted them down, assigning me responsibility for resolving some concerns while he took on the rest. The real terrors—sailing in the ocean at night, or John suffering a debilitating injury or heart attack at sea—were so frightening that when I could bring myself to mention them, my mouth and throat were almost too dry to speak. John had no good answers, either, other than a faith that it would work out.

John had worked at his current advertising agency for fifteen years when a Korean conglomerate purchased it during the merger frenzy of the 1990s. John had advanced through earlier shake-ups, but now he was out of a job. He had large blocks of time to devote to the boat and worked on freelance market research projects as I did. To help fund our trip, we intended to continue working sporadically while we were cruising.

Kate had begged for a dog, and we thought that if we couldn't provide a sibling as a sailing companion, at least we could find a dog. We researched breeds and chose a Portuguese water dog, reputed to be an excellent swimmer. A breeder in Fairfield invited us to meet a new litter of puppies. The breeder's daughter had named the puppies for Sesame Street characters. Long-legged, curly-haired, chocolate-brown, amber-eyed spirited Elmo, the first of the litter to escape the crate, became ours.

When Kate was in second grade, we revealed our plans to her, friends, and relatives. Since we had vaguely talked about it for twenty years, I hadn't anticipated the extent of the shock we would cause. I had my fears to contend with, but now I had to reassure others that we would be safe. John's sister Pat, terrified to lose her young niece at sea, offered to keep Kate while John and I pursued our crazy dream.

Relatives and friends grilled us about pirates, guns, and storms. John assured everyone that he had no desire to confront pirates or sail through hurricanes. We would stay in port if bad weather threatened and avoid areas where pirates struck. We seriously considered purchasing a gun but decided against it. We didn't want to chance an accident.

We didn't talk much about our mutual fear of sailing at night. In over twenty years of sailing, John and I had rarely sailed at night, and the times we had were not reassuring. Sometimes on *Phaedrus*, we had slowly returned to the harbor after a day's sail and in the dark, the profusion of navigation lights from the Connecticut shoreline looked like a randomly twinkling light show. I would frantically examine the charts to figure out which combination of blinking lights matched the Stamford harbor entrance while on the helm, John would maneuver to keep us off the rocks. Then there were the night trips on a friend's boat when our friend would invite acquaintances from New York City bars to sail. As they egged him on, rotted boat parts would let loose and fly off in the dark. One time, a heavy wood block struck John in the head. But we had always made it through.

John urged me to learn to dock the boat, but I refused, which baffled him. Looking back, while I never put forward a strong case for not going cruising or fully expressed my fears, my resistance took other forms. Years after we returned from the voyage, John told me that he was afraid that if he shared any of his doubts, I would pounce, so he kept up a steady drumbeat of enthusiasm.

I would wake up in the middle of the night sweating as shadowy images of mountainous waves crashed down on me. John thought we just needed the experience to overcome our nighttime fears. When I eventually accepted that John intended to go and I had no way out, I called Dr. R., my former psychiatrist. Dr. R. was not the kind of person to charge across the sea. He had a home in Westchester County and an office in Manhattan. I blurted out our cruising plans in the somber tones of someone marching to her death.

Dr. R. was curious about what the boat was like, where we would go first, what we would do for Kate's schooling.

He did not demonstrate the alarm I expected. He said, "Change can be positive."

I ordered Kate's schoolbooks from Calvert, a school in Maryland that offered a program popular among cruising families and child actors. I liked the structure: blocks of twenty lessons with a test at the end of each, which we would send to a teacher at Calvert for grading and comments.

As our departure neared, I gripped the conventional mom role even more fiercely. When a new girl in Kate's class invited her over after school, I drove through familiar streets to pick up Kate. While admiring the fall colors, the carved pumpkins on front stoops, the witch stickers in windows, I complimented myself on how well we fit in Fairfield. As I approached the girl's shabby rental home, I pitied her and her single mom, who had just moved to Fairfield from Boston and didn't know anyone. However, in a few weeks, Kate and I would be as adrift as the girl and her mother.

My days took on a dreamlike quality. I vacillated between wondering if it was too late to bow out and amazement that we would pull it off. John hired Cliff, a licensed captain who had installed our new autopilot, to accompany him on the first leg from Connecticut to Annapolis, Maryland, where they would leave the boat while we finished moving out of the house in Connecticut.

I stayed home to dispose of the furniture and pack. When John and I bought the house, each of our parents—his father, my mother—were moving to small apartments, and we had been the beneficiaries of furniture that they could no longer use. Now we would store favorite pieces and sell the rest. We would add the profits to the cruising kitty.

While John and Cliff sailed *Laughing Goat* to Annapolis, I held a furniture sale. Two women who owned an estate sale company picked over our furniture with their antique and consignment shop cronies while I hid in my basement office, avoiding the people bargaining over the furniture.

At the end of the day, I opened the door to an empty hallway. As I burst into the living room, a man leaning back on one of the remaining chairs held up a glowing blue vase and glanced inquiringly at the two women. The screen door in front clicked shut on the last of the buyers.

Mexican masks, John's African spears, a large painting of Raegan's, and pale blue and rose silk curtains adorned the walls behind him. The man and the women looked out of place in my living room. As they glanced around greedily, I thought of John now sailing *Laughing Goat* down to Annapolis, of Kate finishing up her last days at school, of myself leaving so much behind—and snapped at the man, "I love that vase. I'm keeping it."

John called on the ship's radio from the Chesapeake & Delaware Canal. His excitement crackled over the static and excited me, too. He recounted the lump in his throat when they sailed past the majestic Manhattan skyline, where both of us had spent so much of our professional lives. From out at sea, Atlantic City glowed with flashes of emerald, amber, and ruby lighting up the night.

As the time of our departure closed in, the manic activity took over—packing, dealing with the rest of the furniture, purchasing supplies, and finishing up work projects. Pat helped me pack. We spent a leisurely hour in the kitchen discussing spices, holding up each spice jar to reminisce about the dishes I had made with it, and to decide whether it should be thrown out or given away. The pleasurable conversation abruptly ended when we realized that it was time to pick Kate up from her last day at school. In a frenzy, we tossed the microwave, toaster, and remaining dishes into the dumpster and dashed out, leaving the rest of the house for later.

I picked up Kate in her classroom. The class followed us out onto the sunny lawn, waving and shouting, "Bye, Kate!" as we walked to the car. The October wind shook the tall trees, and Kate's name echoed through the upper branches in the high sweet tones of her classmates. While we sailed, their excited voices would weave through my dreams.

John came home from Annapolis. On the last October Sunday, a sunny Indian summer day, we left our house in Fairfield to move onto *Laughing Goat*. While John loaded the U-Haul van, I cleaned the house. Dust balls floated around the empty bedrooms. I was running out of time when Janet, Kate's best friend Emily's mom, came for Kate's turtle that she had agreed to keep. Looking around at the mess, Janet grabbed a broom, and we tore through the house, sweeping clouds of dust into garbage bags.

We finished in the nick of time, as the renters pulled up. A quick goodbye to Janet and John and Kate climbed in the van while I ran to our Honda with Elmo and Itty Bitty in their respective carriers. I followed the van to Pat's, where we would unload some boxes and bid another farewell. Our departure, planned for years, felt hasty.

John and I sat in the living room with Pat and Fred while Kate and her cousins played. The adults didn't say much. My throat was closed so tight it hurt to speak. Fred had served in the Navy and couldn't believe we didn't know exactly where we were going or where we would wind up. He had lived in Connecticut all his life. He said, "You're giving up a lot."

I couldn't say goodbye. I told myself that we would see each other soon. I wanted to rush to the house in Fairfield and move back in.

As I drove south on I-95 toward Annapolis behind the van that held John, Kate, and the boxes, I caught Elmo's questioning gaze in the rear-view mirror. His amber eyes, which had unnerved me when we first got him, now implored me to explain myself.

"I agree, Elmo, what are we doing here?"

We arrived at the outskirts of Annapolis at around ten o'clock at night and found a motel that accepted pets. The car bumped over the curb as I parked. I could not see or smell the sea.

I wanted to be in my bed in Fairfield in the dove-gray bedroom with the shining brass bedstead. We tumbled into our room in a nondescript lodging on the edge of town, harsh pink lights blinking through the curtains. John said, "Things will look better in the morning."

Chapter Eight
Aboard

When it comes to boat trips, one of the most useful habits that any captain can have is to keep a detailed log. Logs were once used not only as a captain's private journal but also as a detailed account of every aspect of the boat, crew, and journey. Before the world was fully mapped and the ability to position oneself longitudinally was possible, logs often provided the only clues on the course that was necessary to a specific location... The benefits of keeping a good log continue to be beneficial even in the days of GPS and satellite positioning. A log should be kept in a place where it is easy to grab while underway and either write or read and should have its own designated writing instrument assigned to it to make writing quick and easy to do. A waterproof case is helpful and can be as simple as a plastic bag.

—https://www.getmyboat.com/resources/tips-for-owners/454/why-and-how-to-keep-a-ships-log

When our entourage arrived at the boatyard the next morning, *Laughing Goat* sat serenely in a slip on an old wooden dock. Sunlight glinted on the varnished rails and oiled teak deck. Fishing boats chugged in and out of the harbor.

I took in the wood rail, gleaming hatches, chrome fittings, and sparkling blue hull, which John always called flag blue. At first, I thought he had named it himself to distinguish it from more mundane blues like royal or navy, but he was being precise. We used Awl Grip paint, and "Flag Blue" was the color—the dark blue of the deep ocean, midnight blue. An elegant thin gold stripe ran the length of the boat just under the rail.

The wheel, about twice the size of a car steering wheel, was in the center of the cockpit at the stern. On summer days with little wind, I would lie back on the settee and steer with my foot, peeking up occasionally to make sure the boat would not hit anything.

Laughing Goat had roughly 400 square feet of living space below—she was forty-three feet long and twelve feet wide. Our house in Fairfield had 1800 square feet. People had asked me how I could move into such a small space, but when we were sailing, *Laughing Goat* never felt small. On a sunny day on a quiet, winding river in Annapolis, I imagined sailing on and on to the white sandy beaches of the tropics.

John interrupted my reverie. After contemplating the jam-packed van parked behind us, he turned and pointed to *Laughing Goat's* waterline. "If we fill the boat up with all this stuff, the waterline will be below the water. We'll be too heavy to sail."

We had already shed so many belongings. I wanted John to congratulate me on how well I had done selling our things, not crack the whip to sort more, but he was pulling boxes out of the van. I agonized over each item. Elmo, tied to a tree nearby, yawned. John plowed through the boxes, too, holding up particularly ridiculous items like my clunky office fax machine, too big for a boat and useless at sea. Eventually, a mound of boots, bond paper, office machines, and heavy winter clothes lay next to the dumpster.

We had intended Elmo, now six months old, as a companion for Kate, but he became John's dog and followed him everywhere. Portuguese water dogs were originally bred as working dogs along the Portuguese coast to help fishermen herd fish into nets. When we first brought Elmo home, my brother-in-law Fred took in his chocolate brown hair, soulful eyes, and serious demeanor, and called him "the man in the brown suit." Elmo saw Kate as a rival for John's affections and chewed her stuffed animals.

As we finished unloading the van, a girl around Kate's age rode her bike over. She lived on a trawler on the next dock. She and Kate sprinted to the water's edge. John and I nodded to each other, pleased that Kate had already found a friend.

Down below, *Laughing Goat's* compact beauty shone. Teak, mahogany, and brass glowed. Sky-blue cushions covered white settees. Books lined the shelves—*The Ashley Book of Knots, Chapman Piloting & Seamanship, The World's Best Sailboats.* Sunlight poured in through the hatch onto the honey-colored dining table.

At the stern, John's and my sleeping cabin had a queen berth and graceful cabinetry. On a bookshelf next to the berth, I would keep Patrick O'Brien's seafaring novels. His hero, Captain Jack Aubrey, was mine, too, and despite the laughably vast difference between Captain Jack's and my sailing abilities, I emulated his swashbuckling confidence. In Kate's cabin up forward at the bow, she would curl up reading on the V-berth with her beloved stuffed animals or watch a movie on a rabbit-eared TV.

The navigation station across from the galley tucked next to the companionway stairs, held ship's radios, nautical charts, tide tables, John's navigation instruments, parallels and dividers, and the ship's log, a burgundy leather journal with "Yacht Log" and a compass rose embossed in gold on the cover. The thick, cream-colored pages lay blank, waiting for our journey to begin.

The left-hand pages of the log had a line at the top for the name of the vessel and the date, with sixteen lines below to note down the time, position, course, helmsman, current, wind, and weather as the day progressed. The top of the right-hand page was for the passage—where you were leaving from and where you were going. The hopeful destination you jotted down in the morning might be crossed out at the end of the day and replaced with where you actually arrived. The rest of the page was for remarks, comments, and observations.

No matter how tired he was when we arrived at night, John wrote in the log, usually after dinner. He would sit at the navigation station, the desk lamp illuminating the page as his pen scratched across it, Elmo at his feet. Kate and I contributed, too. When I open the log now, I can smell *Laughing Goat*.

On the move-in day in Annapolis, John handed down a few boxes. I put away dishes, filled clear plastic canisters with cereal, pasta, and sugar, and poured Milk Bones into a big plastic jar for Elmo. We threw away the food boxes. Cardboard might harbor roach eggs or disintegrate in the moist air at sea.

On the forward bulkhead in the main cabin, John hung a print from his old office of a fisherman hauling in a line from a trawler's stern on a stormy day. A huge wave was about to hit the bow, yet the fisherman focused on a task, his ruddy face alive with concentration. The print had kept John's spirits up at the agency while he dreamed of sailing. The fisherman's resolute attitude would reassure us at sea, too.

I made up our berth and set a tiny pink porcelain pillbox inscribed with John Masefield's "Sea Fever," a gift from a friend, on the bookshelf. In the main cabin, I arranged a needlepoint pillow that Raegan had made for John's birthday on the settee, along with a pillow from a friend inscribed with the motto, "old friends are the best friends." I put away plates and a serving platter from home, painted with bright blue fish.

John dragged sail bags with an extra genoa, a spinnaker, and a storm trysail through the main salon. Carrying the plastic bin that would be the cat's litter box, I followed him. He jammed the heavy bags into the shower stall.

"Can't you find another place for those?" I asked, hoping to use the shower later.

"It's just temporary. There's no other space for them right now."

Despite all the lockers and cabinets throughout the boat, the sails were too big to fit and needed airflow to avoid mildew. I shoved the litter box next to the sails. Little did I know how hard it would prove to dislodge the sail bags from the shower during the voyage.

Late in the afternoon, Kate bounded down the companionway with her new friend. The girls raced into Kate's cabin up forward and delved into a box of stuffed animals on the V-berth. It was getting towards dinnertime. I stacked the remaining boxes from the galley and main cabin out of the way, vowing to work on them the next day. I grabbed John's mother's old spaghetti pot—somewhere along the way, I had lost the top—and began fixing dinner.

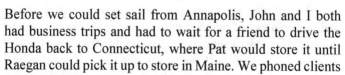

Before we could set sail from Annapolis, John and I both had business trips and had to wait for a friend to drive the Honda back to Connecticut, where Pat would store it until Raegan could pick it up to store in Maine. We phoned clients from an old booth in the boatyard.

We had naively expected warm weather south of the Mason-Dixon line, a taste of the tropical paradise to come. Instead, snow and sleet greeted us in the mornings. The temperature plummeted into the thirties. John worried about the rivers icing up. We bought two small electric heaters.

When the schoolbooks arrived, Kate and I ripped off the packing tape and dove into the box, drinking in the new-book smells. The large-print reading anthology had Disney animals on the cover. We eyed it warily. Kate, an avid reader, no longer read picture books. She disappeared into her cabin with it.

From the time she was a baby, I had read Kate to sleep at night. After we moved on the boat, though, Kate interrupted me, ostentatiously turning pages before I was finished, and saying, "Faster, Mom." After a few nights of rushed readings, she said, "I'm sorry, Mom, but I'd like to read the books myself." Rejected and hurt, I lay next to her reading a different book. She was growing up, ready for chapter books on her own now.

Kate read the second-grade anthology all afternoon. Over dinner, I asked her what she thought. She liked a couple of stories but dismissed most of them as "dumb, for kindergartners." She continued reading into the night. By the end of the following day, she had finished the reading for the entire school year. She returned to her stash of chapter books, which we replenished at a bookstore in town.

To prepare for the first day of school, I reviewed the day's lesson. Looking ahead, I noted that the lessons continually rehashed whatever had gone before. I was surprised to see a grammar book in second grade and hoped that the drudgery of learning grammar would not hinder Kate's love of reading.

Armed with my science illustrations on a large drawing pad and an array of books, I called Kate to the main salon to start our first day of school. Kate wanted to finish a letter she was writing to Emily. Eventually, she sat at the table and opened her notebook. She had labeled neon-colored tabs for every subject and had sharpened pencils. I opened the teacher's guide.

Kate's opinion of the reading material hadn't changed from her earlier assessment—"dumb." We moved uneventfully through science and geography. I was pleased that each subject was modestly interesting.

Then came math. Kate hated it, and it wasn't my favorite, either. She balked at practicing the multiplication tables, a hint of the math fights that would erupt as the school year advanced. At lunchtime, we broke for the day.

The old-fashioned tone and question-and-answer format of the textbooks were deadening. As I gathered the books, I remembered Kate's disappointment after her first day at kindergarten in Fairfield. She had anticipated school for days, brimming with excitement for her first school bus ride. When she returned home a few hours later, her shoulders slumped, she said, "I put on my backpack, get on the bus, go to school, come home, and I have to do this for *100 days*?"

On the boat now, I put the books away and sighed. When I went up north for a work project, John and Kate skipped school. They visited the Naval Academy and a French restaurant where Kate discovered she loved the duck. When John was up north for a presentation, Kate and I foraged through bookstores, and Kate played with her friend, who also didn't seem to go to school.

One day, Kate and I drove around looking at charming houses topped with widows' walks, and she pointed out a house we could buy near a pretty elementary school. I told John that Kate wanted to move to Annapolis and go to school there, and he became even more distressed at our lack of forward movement.

When John prodded me about leaving, though, I would find reasons to linger—letters to mail, cooking ingredients I needed, or tasks on the boat list to finish. John tended towards Cliff's view: when the task list was seventy percent complete, get moving. The longer we stayed in port, the longer the task list grew.

I liked Annapolis. Shopkeepers set out dog bowls on their stoops. Cute restaurants, shops, and bookstores abounded. Kate had a friend. As we continued south, a pattern would emerge: John had to pry me out of towns I liked. I pretended I was a local and resisted leaving.

After four weeks in Annapolis, John and I bundled up in winter jackets and untied the dock lines at dawn three days before Thanksgiving. We pulled into the channel, and I ran below to check on Kate, still in bed. She rubbed and warmed my hands under the covers.

As we got underway, I logged the first entry on November 23, 1996, from Annapolis to Solomon Island in Chesapeake Bay:

Perfect undocking in Annapolis... Kate is cozy under blankets in her cabin... Nice, brisk, sunny... It feels like Long Island Sound, even down to the crab pots. I feel like Miss Marple Goes to Sea, comparing everything to Long Island Sound...

We were off!

Chapter Nine
Chesapeake Bay to Beaufort, North Carolina

In Chesapeake Bay, I anticipated crab dinners fragrant with garlic and butter in homey restaurants. We docked for the night in Solomon Island, a center for crab fishing, at an old wharf alongside dinged-up fishing boats. We strolled the dark streets searching for a restaurant, but the restaurants were shuttered for the season.

The sinking temperature prompted us to hurry back to the boat. As usual, John strode ahead, forging his path. Whether in Manhattan or Solomon Island, John took the streets at a fast clip. When we were first together, I would scramble to keep up. But if I lagged far behind, he would stop, light a cigarette, and wait. I became used to him ahead of me, leaning against a doorway or under an overhang, the tip of his cigarette glowing.

Back on the boat, Kate logged her assessment of Solomon Island:

It's like a dumpster behind McDonalds.

The next night, we stopped at Milford Haven, billed in the cruising guide as a luxurious yacht club. As *Laughing Goat* neared the worn wooden dock, a couple of wiry bay men with missing teeth materialized to catch our lines. They grunted disapprovingly at our angle of approach. When we asked for directions to town, they pointed vaguely and sauntered off.

We explored the deserted grounds. The locked run-down buildings had not been luxurious for decades. A cold mist enveloped us. A blond girl about Kate's age appeared with her grandfather, the two of them vivid against the gray surroundings. The girls played until the girl and her grandfather left, vanishing into the fog.

At dusk, John broke out his new fold-up cruising bike to head to town for chocolate bars. Dwarfing the under-sized wheels, he whirred into the haze, honking the tinny horn like a clown at the circus. Dogs barked in the distance. A few moments later, John exploded back through the murk. He had not found the town and had to fend off the local mutts. We retired to a quiet night of spaghetti and card games on the boat. So far, the Chesapeake Bay of our imaginations was not materializing.

The next day, bright and clear, we headed for Norfolk, an enormous harbor with a Navy base. Wrapped in our winter jackets with the wind on the beam, we admired the fall colors at the shoreline and the skipjacks, local boats designed for Chesapeake Bay. As we approached Norfolk channel, John went below to check the charts and figure out where in the enormous harbor we could stay for the night. At the helm, I fixated on a black channel buoy. It looked odd, a latticework of tubes and wires.

"John, take a look at this. I think this buoy is moving."

"It can't be. Stay the course," he yelled from the nav station, as the black thing zigzagged through the water. Channel markers were supposed to be fixed in place to guide you safely into the harbor.

"Get up here. I don't know what this is. It's moving," I

shouted.

"Shut up! I've got to figure this out. Just keep on course."

The black thing zoomed out of the water, attached to a gray hump. A uniformed Navy captain reared up from the deep like a glowering sea dragon. It happened so fast that as he ascended, I thought he was standing outside on a smooth, shiny gray deck instead of inside the bridge of a submarine.

The captain glared and blasted his horn. He seemed only inches away. A massive roar shook the air, shattering the sunny space and sucking us into a wave of sound. John shot up on deck. The captain blasted the horn again. I yanked the wheel to port.

"Good job, Mom," Kate said.

We both attacked John for telling me to shut up, which he maintained he hadn't done. Still, he hadn't listened to me.

John's version of sailing into Norfolk:

We screamed into Norfolk!

With successes come setbacks. Namely, I mistook a submarine conning tower to be a starboard buoy entrance marker. Looked a bit funny. Big tall black thing with a red top and lots of antennae. But this was Norfolk. And anyway, I was more concerned with the tug coming at us and finding the rest of the entry. Susan said, I vaguely heard, something about the buoy moving <u>at us</u>. *She claims I said shut up. I believe I said, "I'll check on it in a moment, darling."*

Then...the loudest blasts of a horn you'll ever hear. The buoy had grown...immense and steaming at us. Susan managed to turn to port before her heart attack. Kate and I were speechless, struck dumb.

Then...it goes on...a Darth Vader aircraft carrier decides to come out—so that's what all the helicopters were about—at the point where it looks physically impossible to fit in the same harbor, much less the same channel. Dog is going nuts...Kate refused to look until it's almost past. Huge, black, deadly, terrifying.

And so, the rubes from Long Island Sound passed

through the Chesapeake into Norfolk Harbor.

We arrived in Great Bridge, Virginia, our first stop on the Intracoastal Waterway (ICW), a system of rivers and bays linked by manmade canals along the Atlantic Coast from Maine to Florida. The Intracoastal Waterway, a navigable inland route, protected boats from the open ocean's winter storms, which we had no intention of facing. The ICW would take much longer than sailing on the outside, but we did not have the experience to sail on our own for days at a time in the wintry Atlantic. I looked forward to the small towns and pretty marshes of the coastal South.

The next morning, Thanksgiving Day, I huddled near one of the heaters in the main salon, sipping coffee. John hacked away with his machete at the ice on the dock lines. I took out a chicken to defrost. I wanted to roast a turkey, but the oven was too small. Kate thought the chicken was ridiculous.

"It's so tiny." Kate squinted to examine it.

I grabbed my jacket. Stepping onto the dock, I slid across the ice to John, who was taking a break.

"It doesn't feel like Thanksgiving," I said.

At a phone booth attached to the dock office, I called Pat, in her house in Vermont, where we normally spent Thanksgiving together. One of her daughters picked up. I could hardly hear her over the racket in the background. I imagined Pat checking the turkey, and Fred creaming onions. I would have been sautéing spinach. Her daughter told me that the house was crowded, and we weren't missing anything. Still, I longed to be there.

"Where are you? What is it like?" she asked.

"Different," I said.

I told her about our approach to Norfolk when the submarine zoomed out of the water and blasted the horn so loud the air shook. I explained our frustration when approaching drawbridges. We didn't understand the thick southern accents of the bridge tenders and couldn't get them to open the bridges for us. We suspected that the New York port of call emblazoned on the hull encouraged them to give the Yankees a hard time. I told her about the mysterious bright white line on the water that snaked around a bend in the river and then suddenly rose and flew off—hundreds of geese in V formation.

Pat got on the phone. Before calling, I had imagined her fierce anger at us for leaving, her inconsolable sorrow at losing us. When we left, she had bemoaned the fact that she would be the last Russell sibling living in Connecticut. Now, she exuded good cheer.

"How's Kate?" she asked.

"She's writing a novel, and John rigged up a swing for her on the end of a halyard that she loves. She misses Emily, though."

Kate wrote daily postcards to her best friend, Emily, but most of them were not mailed because we weren't staying anyplace long enough to send them. Kate swooped over the water on her swing in long, slow arcs from bow to stern. She said she got ideas for writing that way. She was working on a novel about a young girl, Kristi, and her adventures trapping animals. John and I were on the lookout for boats with kids.

After I hung up with Pat, the sun peeked out. The day warmed up, and the ice thawed. Later, we had an early dinner of chicken and squash and green beans. After dinner, John, Elmo, and I checked out the other boats along the dock while Kate changed into her pajamas. There was a boat from Holland on a trip through the States and a catamaran heading down to Palm Beach.

When we had been traveling for a week, Kate asked how much farther it was to Florida, the jumping-off point to the Bahamas, our first offshore destination.

"About a thousand miles," John said.

"One thousand? How fast do we go?"

"Six -knots an hour."

John explained that a knot was equal to a little over a mile. Despite Kate's dislike of math, she quickly figured that it would take a long time. On the Intracoastal Waterway, cars and trucks whizzed by on roads in the distance. Planes flew overhead out of Norfolk.

"So, it will take us weeks and weeks, and we could have driven or flown? You chose the slowest way to travel," she said, shaking her head incredulously.

My days were busy on the Intracoastal Waterway—preparing for the day's run, navigating, looking out for tree stumps in the channel, and doing schoolwork with Kate. I rose early to brew coffee. We sipped it in the cockpit, admired the sunrise, and studied the marine charts.

John and I would look at each other for a moment before he started the engine.

John said, "Here goes nothing."

If I blurted out something hopeful like "The engine's been doing great!" before he cranked it, John's withering glance would quiet me. He didn't want any jinxes. He would turn the engine over and if it went without a hitch, he might say, "Better than a sharp stick in the eye."

John had a trove of sayings from his mother, now long passed. When he uttered one, I could feel his mother's reassuring, jocular presence. Don't take anything for granted, don't take yourself too seriously.

We warmed the engine while we went about boat tasks—getting sails ready, cleaning, and stowing loose items, all the while listening for anything out of place. We had become attuned to any shift in engine noise, or any change at all—the small bump on the hull before we became stuck hard aground, the flutter of the telltales as the wind shifted into an unexpected squall. Kate had become a hypersensitive listener, too, sometimes yelling out warnings from her cabin while half-asleep.

In Coinjock, North Carolina, we had our first taste of

Southern hospitality. The marina owners had four dogs and offered to watch Elmo while they loaned us their van to get barbecue at a local joint. We inhaled the intoxicating smoky smells as we ordered at the bar and sat down at one of the small, scuffed tables. Everyone called us "honey." As Seinfeld played on TV in the background, we ate ribs and hush puppies. This was heaven. We never wanted to leave.

One night we anchored in a narrow bend in the Alligator River Canal, surrounded by dense woods so close that we could have jumped on land from the boat. Gnarly misshapen trees cast gloomy shadows over us. John worried about becoming stuck on a shoal as the boat swung on the anchor during the night, or worse, getting murdered by sly locals:

...We're fine unless we're eaten by a water moccasin or bear or killed by one of the toothless bay men who might have been tailing us from Milford Haven.

Forecast for tonight is increasing winds from the south/southeast to 35 by tomorrow. Lord, I'm unhappy about this. I'm sure the night will be fitful...

John stayed up all night in the cockpit humming the tune from *Deliverance*. He held onto an emergency flare, ready to defend us from marauders. When I woke up in the morning, he was still sitting there, eyes pleading wordlessly to save him from his hellish fantasies.

It took us twelve days to go from Annapolis, Maryland, to Beaufort, North Carolina, on the Intracoastal Waterway—about four hundred miles on the highway. On good days, we enjoyed sunny weather, leaping dolphins, flocks of birds silhouetted against glorious sunsets, and fabulous Southern cooking. Other days, though, when we suffered through gales or freezing rain, ran aground, or were stuck in port altogether, Kate and I would crawl into our bunks with books while John pored over cruising guides.

We arrived in Beaufort in time for John to leave on a business trip to New York. After two weeks on the move, I looked forward to a few days of vacation exploring the quaint town with Kate. John tied extra dock lines in case bad weather struck while he was away, kissed us goodbye, and headed for the airport.

Chapter Ten
Beaufort to West Palm Beach

With John away, we skipped school. Kate played with her collection of My Little Ponies, issuing bossy commands, or whispering secrets to pink and purple fillies while I puttered about the main cabin. We would go out to lunch at a diner across the road, packing a deck of cards and a couple of books.

One night while John was still in New York, the wind began to blow hard. Kate thought the boat was tipping over. As I mulled over the situation, trying to shut out the howling wind and some unpleasant grinding noises, Kate asked, "Aren't you going to do anything?"

She wasn't alarmed, just interested. If I were alone on the boat, I might have eked out another hour or two, hoping the storm would wear itself out before I had to deal with it. But I felt I had to do something because of Kate.

I ventured out. It was pitch black. Rain pelted down and

waves crashed into the dock. I looked up and down the long dock and saw no one, just a line of boats wildly careening around the slips. Foaming white waves crested at the harbor entrance and cascaded toward me.

I jumped on the slippery dock. The fenders, which protected the boat from the dock, were out of position. I tried to shove the fenders back in place but couldn't move the boat against the fifty-knot gusts and pummeling waves, which banged *Laughing Goat's* gleaming hull and expensive new paint job against the dock. I wasn't sure what to try next.

I hooked up our phone cable to another boat's phone line, called John, and told him what was happening. Through the static, I imagined him about to go out for dinner at his favorite restaurant near a friend's apartment where he was staying.

"The lines are all holding? You'll be fine," he said cheerily, trying to reassure me. He didn't hear my desperation.

I struggled to get the fenders back in place but still couldn't move the boat against the wind. In all the years of sailing with John, I had not handled any situations like this on my own; we had done it together. When an older man hurried by to his boat across from us, I asked for help. Grumbling, he pushed the boat off, and a few inches of space opened between the boat and the dock into which I shoved the fenders.

Within an hour, I heard grinding again. The fenders had slipped. I knocked on my grumbling neighbor's boat. He opened it a crack, and I asked if he would help.

"No," he said and shut the door.

Floored at the lack of neighborly kindness, I stomped across the dock. Bracing myself with my back to the piling for leverage and feet pressed along the cabin sole, I pushed *Laughing Goat* away from the dock as my neighbor had and crammed in a boat cushion and two fenders. I stayed on watch during the night until the wind died down and stuffed the cushion in whenever it moved.

When I woke in the morning, the sun was out. A minor scratch remained on the hull, but otherwise the boat was fine. I crowed about my success to John when he arrived home that night. Still, when I looked at the scratch, I wondered if I would have managed, had conditions worsened. John trusted me to take care of the boat. Whenever I did, though, my resentment flared up that John hadn't been there when I needed him. I counted on John being there for me.

One night in Beaufort, we were eating dinner below when we heard strains of Jimmy Buffett crooning on loudspeakers. We rushed on deck where sailboats glided past us, lights twinkling in the shrouds, garish plastic Santas and fake palm trees swinging from masts—an enchanting, laid back, Southern take on Christmas.

In Beaufort, John had a worklist to complete:

Gadget for inspection plate, clean bilge, change fuel filters, windlass switch, bilge pump hose screen, buy new Par pump as back-up, check fuel levels, check running on separate tanks—current practice is to run with both lines open.

I had to provision the boat for five days when we anticipated reaching the next large town. As John and I finished our tasks, Elmo, now a one-year-old puppy, made himself at home in Beaufort. He trotted to nearby boats for treats. Despite his lack of obvious virility—chocolate brown curly hair, amber eyes, and a prance—Elmo was a magnet for Southern men, and John, who normally avoided small talk, chatted on the dock for hours with Elmo's admirers.

John urged me to hurry. It was eight hundred miles to West Palm Beach, where he would prepare the boat for offshore sailing. The longer we dithered in Beaufort, the greater the delay in departing Florida, and we would miss the weather opportunity to cross to the Bahamas.

On a blustery day, we left Beaufort and headed to Charleston before the next cold front blasted through. We eased into a travel rhythm. John noted that the landscape was "a series of ditches but with birds everywhere"—marshy land dotted with graceful egrets and herons. Our focus narrowed to the numbers on the depth sounder as we nosed the boat back and forth through the canals to avoid the shallows. At night, we docked in small towns or anchored in the marshes. On the way to Wrightsville, we went aground twice. Passing Camp LeJeune, we heard shots in the distance and waved to Marines.

During school time, which we had cut down to two or three days a week, Kate and I fought over math. Initially, John tried to intervene. Our battles perplexed him, but Kate and I ignored him. It was *our* battleground. The primary battle erupted over multiplication tables, with minor skirmishes over the review problems at the end of each chapter. We covered other subjects relatively smoothly, but when I insisted that Kate practice the tables, she refused.

"Okay, Kate, let's do fours. What're four times two?"

Kate would roll her eyes or draw. I felt guilty that we'd spirited Kate from a school in which she had thrived. I didn't see the point of all the memorization, either, but on we went.

As we sailed further south, John's and my anxiety increased about offshore sailing. When we imagined departing Florida, we pictured the ocean floor dropping thousands of feet and the water becoming charcoal blue, almost black, in places like Tongue of the Ocean or the Puerto Rico Trench, the deepest spot in the Atlantic. As John read into the night to prepare for offshore sailing, he would lean toward me at odd moments and whisper, "Puerto Rico Trench." I'd scream involuntarily. He'd laugh, but he scared himself, too.

John described our bedraggled entry through the rain to Charleston:

Left McClellanville 8:30 a.m., arrived Charleston about 4 p.m. One extremely miserable day…Cold in a.m., then rainy and cold in p.m. Generally made good time going through the "low country" marshes with their little rivers and inlets. Very pretty country. By the time we got to the

Ashley River, it had been raining for a bit; we were tired, very wet. Dog was miserable but looked very funny with his wet hair, etc. Susan by this time looks like she wants to kill me. She wanted to bail at the Ben Sawyer Bridge, but I knew tomorrow would be worse. So, we go anyway. Raining, so we can't see the charts or the marks, I'm so cold I'm beginning to jump involuntarily...but I know only a short hop to the docks once we're through Charleston harbor. All I kept thinking was...God! I'm glad we're not doing this on the outside!

John's mantra: so, we go anyway.

I had become used to John's tenacity when he worked on *Laughing Goat*. Watching John at the helm as Charleston came into view, his face grim, rain dripping off his hat and jacket, teeth chattering, I was glad he had persisted, and we were not stuck in the muddy canals for another night. In the pouring rain, a cheerful dockhand caught the dock lines and welcomed our grumpy crew to Charleston, where we would spend Christmas.

At the dock in Charleston, we strung multicolored lights up the rigging and decorated the main cabin with red chili pepper lights. John observed that the blinking red interior resembled a Texas whorehouse and declared it a success. Bundled in winter jackets, we biked through Charleston complaining about the cold. John noted:

Has been extremely cold, lows in 20s, but it's a nice town. Very human scale architecture, like London in a funny way. Spirits of the crew are poor. Christmas coming, and missing home Susan. Kate...unhappy... I'm short-tempered and scream at Kate or the cat periodically.

On Christmas Day, we exchanged presents, called home, and went out for a nice dinner, but we were ready to leave the charming, damp city behind. Two days later, we headed out through a tranquil stretch of delicate, sandy marshes.

The temperature warmed, and dolphins appeared. We pulled into our last stop in South Carolina, Daufuskie Key, a little island near the Georgia border. In the waning light of sunset, a family of dolphins frolicked, and we shook off the Christmas blues.

On St. Simon's Island in Georgia, we met a family who planned to go cruising the following year with two girls near Kate's age. They peppered us with questions and invited Kate to spend the night on their boat. John and I had our first night off in two months since the trip began.

Decked out in a dress, jewelry, and make-up, I sashayed down the dock, and we had dinner in a restaurant on the water. After dinner, John took my hand as we strolled the docks and admired the features we coveted on newer sailboats. John said how pretty I looked with my blue-and-gold earrings and necklace glinting in the waning sun.

"We should make a point of going out more often," he said, squeezing my bare shoulder and pulling me towards him. Leaning into him, I agreed.

On the way to St. Augustine, Florida, we sailed in the Atlantic. For the first time, we turned on the new autopilot. Like magic, the boat steered herself. In deep water, we didn't have to worry about steering around shoals every few seconds, as we did on the Intracoastal Waterway. With the sun out and mild weather, my fears about crossing to the Bahamas lifted, and I read aloud from Bahamas' cruising guides. As I emoted, John asked me to tone it down. My newfound zeal ramped up his anxiety about the crossing.

In Titusville, a herd of manatees, playful but alarming, converged on the dinghy, thudding against it. At the dock, they wriggled on their backs, while Kate joined a gaggle of children who sprayed water over their bellies.

We had run into very few children so far on the trip. One boy who lived on a boat in Charleston and wore a purple cape had flung himself at Kate from behind pilings on the dock while shouting unintelligibly. She had wanted nothing to do with him. John urged Kate to play with the children in

Titusville, yet we were only there for the afternoon, and the French Canadian children didn't speak English.

In West Palm Beach, John whipped himself along to ready the boat for offshore sailing, but preparations took longer than expected. My mother lived in an apartment complex in Palm Beach, and we swam at her pool, where John taught Kate to snorkel. I tried to ignore my mother's complaints and veiled attacks.

"Oh, is John still smoking? He looks heavy. Kate wrote me a thank-you note, but it was so short. Does she know how to write them?"

I wished that she could just appreciate us.

While John and Kate swam, my mother would fill a five-gallon pail in her sink and ask me to water the plants on the terrace, a jungle of greenery. As I lugged the pail and bent over the plants, my mother complained about her view and about her brother, who owned her apartment and had given it to her to live in but hadn't invited her to a party at his mansion in Palm Beach. I waved to John and Kate in the pool and stared at the blue Atlantic across the road while grinding my teeth.

My mother could not understand how I could have given up the house in Connecticut, a symbol of success, to sail away. When I was with my mother, I saw our voyage through her eyes: a foolish scheme that John concocted, and I had weakly played along. My blood would boil at the imagined scenario. Through clenched teeth, I would defend our trip, exaggerating how much I wanted to go.

I envied John's skill in deflecting my mother with what Raegan called his snide voice of icy WASP politeness. He could shut her down with a look. After seeing her, I would pound the steering wheel of the car in frustration as I drove back to the boat. A day or two would pass before I could shake the reverberations of a visit.

Our preparations continued apace. We installed a new inverter, a wind generator, and a single-sideband radio. We bought a thirty-seven-pound Fortress anchor and chain, a giant fire extinguisher, a sump pump powerful enough to dredge a large swamp, a storm anchor, and a life raft. We could live at sea on the raft for days on emergency protein bars with a tiny water-maker, flares, and a spear gun. I bought large rolls of gauze to stanch big wounds and splints to set bones, filled prescriptions for heavy painkillers and antibiotics, and took another CPR course.

At the store where we bought sixty feet of fire hose, the clerk asked, "What are you buying this for?"

"It's for my boat," John said. "We're going offshore."

"How big is your boat? This could pump out a high school." The clerk smirked as he cut the hose.

"Forty-three feet," John said. He looked away to discourage further conversation. Clerks in every store and supply house had dispensed unwanted advice. John was sticking to his guns. He wasn't going to be the captain whose ship sank for lack of a strong enough pump or the proper hose.

We prepared for the worst eventualities: a fire, sinking, a hurricane, broken bones. Each successive purchase drove home the risks of the venture. Our worries escalated. Were we going to do this? At what point could we declare ourselves ready? My middle-of-the-night thoughts alternated between missing home and visions of *Laughing Goat* tearing across the ocean in the dark as waves crashed over the bow.

John walked Elmo at night in the little park next to the marina. Unlike the friendly docks in Beaufort, the park harbored a ragged crowd of drunks and addicts. Having worked in New York for many years, John usually sprinted through without a hassle. Still, one night, John had to throw rocks at a drunk's dog that attacked Elmo. It was time to leave.

Our trip would be delayed again, however. Itty Bitty, the cat, who usually crouched on a shelf in the back of our sleeping cabin—black fur melting into the darkness, green eyes smoldering as she hissed at Elmo—ventured out on the dock. When we couldn't find her, we thought she might have strayed aboard a rusty Cuban freighter, but the crew hadn't seen her. We combed the docks, the park, and checked the surrounding water.

When she didn't turn up the next day, John and Kate tacked up signs around the neighborhood offering a reward. Kate cried, imagining her kitty lost or drowned. To reassure Kate, we made up stories: Itty Bitty was a stowaway bound for Cuba, or she had joined the gang of feral cats in the park.

We couldn't wait any longer, or we would miss favorable weather to sail to the Bahamas. Taut with anticipation for the offshore sail ahead but unsettled at our carelessness in losing Itty Bitty, we left for Miami, the jumping-off point for the sea voyage. John wrote:

Kate is distraught and sees this either as proof that leaving the red house in Connecticut was one of her father's hare-brained ideas or an omen of things to come. We must make every effort to find the cat. Otherwise, I'm sure Kate will think that if she disappears, we'll just say, "Oh well, tsk tsk"...and keep sailing.

We never did find Itty Bitty.

Chapter Eleven
Sailing to the Bahamas

Ogling the mansions that lined the Intracoastal Waterway, we had an easy run from Palm Beach down to Fort Lauderdale. From there, we sailed out in the Atlantic to Miami while John and I tried to decipher the offshore weather reports, upon which we would soon have to rely.

At sea, we would receive weather reports on the single sideband radio, a recent purchase, which we had not yet learned to use. Close to shore, the VHF radio, much simpler to operate, picked up weather forecasts. At first, as we listened to the offshore forecasts, delivered quadrant-by-quadrant over vast regions of the ocean, and formatted to allow mariners to compare successive reports for slight differences, we stared at each other in mutual incomprehension.

The single-sideband radio was bulky with numerous dials, hundreds of channels, and a tricky antenna. We spent hours finding a good spot for the antenna, poring over the manual, and trying to home in on stations amid crackling, static, wails, and shrieks. After aligning several dials, if we zeroed in on a station, it wheezed in and out. I felt like I was in a 1940s war movie as I twisted the dials.

To sail to the Bahamas, we would cross the Gulf Stream, a warm, fast-moving current flowing north in the Atlantic Ocean, stretching from the Gulf of Mexico through the Florida Straits and up the East Coast. When winds blew from the north opposing the current, huge waves formed, that we had to consider and possibly endure. During a freak March storm in 1993, a well-known Florida restaurateur, an experienced boater, was lost at sea in the Gulf Stream.

John struggled to calculate how long it would take to cross the Gulf Stream, which would dictate the time of departure. The current could cut the boat speed in half. Cruising books recommended leaving at midnight to ensure arriving in good light. If we arrived after dark, we would not see the coral and sandbars at the harbor entrance. We wavered between an early-morning departure and a night crossing.

Another big decision loomed: finding a "weather window." Until this voyage, that phrase had little meaning, but in the Miami marina, guesses of a good weather window echoed from dock to dock. Some sailors hired private weather forecasters. Everyone wanted to sail off at the beginning of two or three days of favorable winds. Though we had at first mocked boaters who went to extravagant lengths to second-guess conditions, as the reality of departure set in, John contacted a professional meteorologist, too.

With other boats at the Miami marina also waiting to cross to the Bahamas, dockside chatter masqueraded as expertise. Many "experts" never left the dock but rehashed maritime accidents in excruciating detail. After a week of scaring ourselves with confusing weather reports and conflicting opinions from dockside experts, we had enough. On a cloudy, breezy day, we listened to the latest weather report. John checked with the meteorologist who covered Caribbean weather for sailors. The next few days looked favorable. In a stupor of anxiety, we returned the rental car, withdrew cash at the ATM, and made final preparations.

We hemmed and hawed, and decided on a ten o'clock evening departure to Gun Cay. We would cross the dreaded Gulf Stream in the middle of the night.

A wiry Englishman from the boat across the dock tossed us the bow line as we pulled out of the slip. His wife stood alongside him, waving cheerfully. He asked where we were headed.

"The Bahamas," John said.

"I hope your trip over is smoother than ours was this afternoon," he shouted as we rounded the dock.

John and I looked at each other. Although fair weather was predicted, clouds obscured the stars. While Kate happily chattered, ready for adventure, we both glanced warily at the channel leading out of the harbor and beyond into impenetrable darkness.

We focused on our usual boat tasks. As we headed out of the marina, John steered, and I coiled lines and tidied fenders. A lighted red buoy marked the turn where we would enter Government Cut, the channel that led into the ocean. Although I had viewed it neutrally in the past among the vast array of lights in this busy port, tonight the blinking red light reminded me of the safety of the inner harbor.

We turned left and entered Government Cut. For about a half-mile or so, red buoys lined the left side of the channel and green ones lined the right. There were no other boats in the normally teeming channel. Beyond the strings of lit buoys—utter blackness.

"What did he mean?" I asked, referring to the Englishman's comment as we left.

"I don't know," John replied. "The weather guy said everything looked good."

Kate's bright chatter ceased. Sensing the tension, she slipped below deck with a book.

"Which marker is that?" John asked, pointing to a green buoy some distance away.

"I think it's '11.' I can't read it." I adjusted the binoculars.

We headed closer to confirm the number. "Do you think he was talking about the Gulf Stream?" I was stuck on the Englishman's words. My teeth chattered.

"Probably." John's blue eyes had shrunk to narrow slits.

"It's '11.'" Only five more pairs of buoys to go, and the boat would disappear into the void ahead. *Laughing Goat* plunged on. John and I were silent.

The boat felt like she was running in slow motion. We passed another pair of buoys. Four to go. I could not look at John. I wanted him to feel certain about embarking on this midnight venture. Was he unsure like I was?

I eventually looked over at my husband. We had never been big talkers. In that way, our relationship was similar to the one I had with my dad, who had always known what I was up to, without much talk about it. Now, although I quickly looked away, I knew John knew what I felt, too.

"Shall we do this?" he asked. He was giving me a way out, which I ached to grab. Three pairs of buoys to go.

But if I snatched it, the recriminations would be endless. I did not want to be the one to make the choice. Yet all our careful reasoning and piles of charts and books could not stand up against the fear now rising in my stomach.

John said quietly, "Let's go back."

"Are you sure?" I asked, even though my body had already pleasantly slackened at the suggestion. I sank onto the cockpit cushion. John had poured so much of himself into this voyage. Turning back would unleash a torrent of self-doubt. He would dismiss all that he had done to get us this far.

He slowly turned the boat around. I became conscious of breathing in and out, of a soft breeze blowing across my body and wafting through the palm trees that swayed gently on the beach against the backdrop of neon-lit South Beach high-rises. We continued back to the marina, toward the tiki bar in the distance where people milled around under yellow lights. Disco music floated across the harbor.

I had wanted to swagger onto the dock at Cat Cay, a Bahamian island across from Gun Cay, where visitors checked in with the immigration authorities. I glanced back to the outer edge of the channel. I could almost make out a ghost ship, carrying a younger version of us, the hippies careening around Long Island Sound on an old wooden ferryboat.

I did not understand how we would get to the Bahamas now, how we could feel any differently tomorrow about heading into the blackness.

John's version of events, which he wrote *after* we crossed successfully:

The non-events of the preceding page, logging the successful crossing, fail to paint the true picture, a romance novel gloss-over of the real terror and shame that led to the Great Gulf Stream Crossing. Four or five days earlier, we had steeled ourselves, armed with days of listening to the offshore broadcast, a fresh read-out from our ace router Walt, nights of teaching myself vector diagrams, the boat prepared, surveyed, equipment lashed, all provisioned. Tanks full, engine checked, and we actually left the dock at about ten p.m. at night.

An oh-so-nice couple helped with the dock lines and tossed, with the lines, a casual comment that they hoped our trip was smoother than the one they had that afternoon. Within a nanosecond, all confidence—which must have been gossamer thin—vanished. Within ten minutes, we were staring out at the channel lights that looked like a neon path to the darkest hell I've ever dreamed.

Kate's chipper chatter and excitement soon evaporated. Spooked by our normal confusion about where the right mark was, "Susan, the green says '11' not '13', where the hell is '13'?"...etc., she bailed... I kept looking

*out the road to hell. The swells became larger. I—for a
second—panicked. Let's bag it. And we did.*

*Oh, the shame! How embarrassing! How the hell do I
expect to sail around the world...*

The next morning in the Miami marina, we sipped
coffee in the cockpit. During the night, John had restlessly
padded around the main cabin and the deck.

"How can we cross oceans if we're afraid of the dark?"
he muttered.

Our British neighbor across the dock sprinted over to
ask what had happened.

"Engine trouble," John said.

Later that morning, John called Cliff, the licensed
captain who had helped John bring the boat down from
Connecticut to Annapolis. Cliff had crossed the Atlantic and
sailed the Mediterranean and Caribbean Seas. Neither of us
wanted to head out again into the blackness alone.

As we waited for Cliff to arrive, the failure to cross on
our own grated. We entertained the idea of telling him not to
come and trying again. John chain-smoked and avoided
people on the dock.

He said, "We can't be such babies. You have to learn
to take a night watch." He had taken night watches on the
trip down to Annapolis with Cliff.

"I will," I said, not exactly seeing how that would
happen, given my record so far.

As John pushed me to overcome my nighttime fear, he
castigated himself. John avidly followed sailing races like
the Southern Ocean Racing Circuit, America's Cup, or the
Fastnet, where crews sailed through extreme weather,
sometimes suffering fatalities. Although John looked like a
born sailor with a craggy face, L.L. Bean sweater, and worn
topsiders, he didn't like sailing at night or in bad weather
much more than I did.

When Cliff arrived, I effusively greeted him. John's
greeting was more restrained. Cliff's presence was a painful
reminder of our cowardice.

A week later, at the "cracka" dawn, as Cliff liked to say, we headed out of Miami, bound for Nassau. Cliff had quickly dispensed with the idea of leaving at night again. He, too, preferred an early morning departure, and with *Laughing Goat's* six-foot three-inch draft, he wanted to stay in deep water to Nassau. We decided to sail through the night north of the Berry Islands to arrive in Nassau the following day. It would be my first overnight sail. Again, we motored out of Government Cut past the tall condo buildings on South Beach.

A couple of hours later, Cliff was below in the nav station while John, Kate, and I were on deck, hoping to spot the Gulf Stream's western wall. The sun hid behind clouds. Deep cobalt blue water stretched to the horizon. Fresh, salty air filled our lungs.

"It looks like we're in the Gulf Stream," Cliff said, noting that our speed had slowed to four knots with the current pushing us north. The change was barely noticeable, though, like crossing a highway into another state. The Gulf Stream, which had loomed so large during our preparations, was tame that day.

Later, I prepared my first dinner at sea, searing steaks in olive oil with garlic and rosemary. I inhaled the pungent smells, reminding me of cooking in the kitchen in Connecticut. Although the seas were gentle, I practiced strapping myself to the stove with a wide white canvas strap meant to keep the cook from toppling over in rough weather.

The moon beamed a wide path on the water. Stars blanketed the sky. Great Stirrup Cay Lighthouse, north of the Berry Islands, glowed faintly in the distance. *Laughing Goat* raced toward it at nine knots, with the current now helping us. The boat swooshed through the darkness.

The light was shining more brightly when I passed out chocolate bars for dessert. I remembered the panic I used to feel as we groped our way toward Stamford Harbor, unsure of where we were. But in this sparsely traveled part of the ocean, there was breathing room. The lighthouse's beam pulsated into the darkness and pointed the way, a lone streetlamp in a corner of the sea. There were still miles to go in deep water.

Later, as we neared the now blazing light, we discerned the shapes of fishing boats. Bathed in the reflected light, men hustled around the decks of the trawlers. They shouted back and forth as they hauled in lines and nets. A large yacht was closing in on us—*fast*—from the other direction. We steered to starboard to give it room as John ran forward, yelling. It, too, veered to starboard, and then sped by on our port side, narrowly missing us.

We discovered that when we had hastily attached our navigation lights after applying a final coat of varnish to the rails before we left, we reversed them. John quickly switched them around. So far, the most dangerous moment on the crossing was this one, and it was our fault.

I went to sleep for a few hours while John stayed on watch. When I woke up, the sky was brightening. I heated water for coffee and groggily headed up on deck. Cliff, now on watch, was smiling, pointing to a low gray mound way off in the distance—New Providence Island, where Nassau was located. I brought up coffee and sat on the forward deck, hugging my knees.

I grinned at Cliff, at *Laughing Goat*, at the mound on the horizon we were heading towards. We were in Northwest Providence Channel, where the Atlantic Ocean fed into the water northwest of New Providence. The vast ocean stretched out in front of me.

I thought of the summer John and I lived aboard *XL* on a mooring out in Mamaroneck Harbor. I had loved waking up in the morning to the sounds of seawater lightly slapping the hull, fishing boats chugging out of the harbor, and seagulls crying. Even then, the voyage we were on now was a gleam in John's eye, a goal that sustained him.

Cruise ships streamed toward Nassau. John woke up and we watched ships and fishing boats disappear into the harbor. As the entrance neared, Kate and I raised the courtesy flag, a small replica of the Bahamian flag. The U.S. flag flew from our stern. When we entered the harbor, tremors of patriotic fervor, which I rarely experienced while in the States, swept through my body.

Low pink, white, and gray buildings lined the Nassau shore. A high bridge arched over the harbor to Paradise Island, where modern resort hotels rose into the sky. On the Nassau side, old wooden wharves jutted out, and workers loaded crates onto hand trucks. Snippets of loudspeaker announcements drifted over the harbor from cruise ships. John called Nassau Harbor Control on the radio.

"Nassau Harbor Control, this is *Laughing Goat*." John's breath caught. I stood near him to witness a historic exchange. We had made it to another country, a dot in the ocean twelve hundred miles from where the voyage began.

"This is Nassau Harbor Control. Switch to channel ten, please."

The clipped British accent thrilled me.

"*Laughing Goat* requests permission to enter the harbor."

He asked John a few questions about how long we were staying and our next port of call and then said, "Permission granted. Welcome to Nassau."

The crisply enunciated syllables echoed through the boat. We had passed the first hurdle.

We pulled into the marina where we had arranged a slip, and raised the bright yellow Q-flag, indicating that we were quarantined to the boat until we cleared customs. Cliff, who had sailed through the Caribbean and crossed the Atlantic, told us the drill: wait patiently, be polite, and offer the officers a cold drink.

Soon, a tall, portly customs officer in a thick khaki uniform knocked on the boat. He pointed to the gate in our lifelines, indicating we should open it so he could climb aboard. In his bulky shoes, he looked like a landlubber. He did not at all resemble my stereotyped fantasy of a Caribbean official whom I had imagined breaking into a reggae song while leaping over the lifelines barefoot.

He heaved himself aboard. John gestured towards the cooler and rattled off drinks as though at a cafe: coke, seltzer, juice, lemonade, beer, and iced tea. The official declined politely, examined the boat papers, stamped our passports, and left. Our relief at cutting through the red tape was short-lived. An immigration officer came next. With the gate now open, he briskly climbed onto the boat and accepted a glass of orange juice. Elmo sniffed his pant cuffs, and the officer froze. I grabbed Elmo, and John hurriedly led the officer below for the next round of questions. After that, we were cleared.

I stepped lightly off the boat. Kate ran toward the rambling collection of one-story pink buildings to explore the pool at the marina. I smiled at a Bahamian woman carrying a pile of tightly folded laundry.

We had sailed *Laughing Goat* across the Gulf Stream and the Florida Straits. A chink had opened up in our knowledge of ourselves and of what we could do. The paralyzing fear that had gripped us in the channel the week before had vanished. But there were no guarantees about crossing from the Bahamas to our next destination.

I jumped in the pool at the marina. Kate and I played a game we had made up, "peaceful back float." I floated in the sunny pool, eyes closed, humming like I hadn't a care in the world until Kate poked me from below, disrupting my tranquility. Later, before Cliff caught a plane back to Connecticut, we went to lunch at a restaurant overlooking the harbor. Over conch fritters and key lime pie, we rehashed the crossing, our words tumbling over each other in our excitement.

After Cliff left, his role in the crossing faded in our retellings, as though we had cut out his image from a photograph. When we regaled people with the story of the crossing, neither of us mentioned Cliff. If anyone had happened to see him in a photo and asked who he was, we would have said he was a friend. Many years after we returned from the voyage, Kate was surprised to learn that Cliff was a hired captain. Over the years, I had forgotten how conflicted we were about his presence.

Chapter Twelve
Cheeseburgers in Paradise

Dear 2C,

I miss you. Sorry I haven't been writing you, but I've been very busy. Did you get my two letters that I've already written? I don't know since you didn't write me.

I'm in Nassau, Bahamas. Dad and I went to swim with stingrays about a week ago on Blue Lagoon Island, which is famous for the movie, 'Splash.' We snorkeled all around the stingrays. Dad took a picture of me in the water.

Yesterday, Mom and I went to swim with dolphins. We swam in about 20 feet of water. The dolphins felt half rubbery-smooth and half-soft. Their top fin doesn't have any bones. If you ride on one, you could damage them for life. I threw a ring for one named Blue, and she came back with it. It was like a dog playing fetch, except she came back with it on her snout. I met the 3 dolphins that starred in Flipper. Three played Flipper because one can't do it the whole two hours. One was named Fatman. He was nine feet long and about 500 pounds. Another was McGyver, and the third was Jake.

About two weeks ago, we tried to cross to Allen's Cay. Big mistake or as Jimmy Buffett would say, 'Big, big mistaka.' The waves were about 5-12 feet. The wind was in our faces as usual. The current was going the wrong way, as usual. My Mom upchucked. I didn't upchuck, but I was miserable because I was afraid to eat anything. My stomach hurt a little, and I couldn't tell if it was from the waves or not. Guess what? It was from hunger. I ate one plum and one banana for lunch.

Then Elmo upchucked all over the cockpit, including on my Dad's precious new binoculars and on my Mom's shorts. There was tons of coral and rocks all around us. We did OK with that. We didn't do OK with the waves, though. They slowed us down so much, we turned back.

From Kate

P.S. Write back. I've written 3 letters and not one from you!!!!!!!!!!!!!!!

When Kate penned her letter to the second-grade class, 2C, in Fairfield, we had been in Nassau for a few weeks while John and I alternated business trips to New York. We had sailed to a land of seven hundred islands, but *Laughing Goat* had yet to leave the dock.

In New York, a sidewalk throng hustled me through midtown while horns blared, and I longed for my quiet life on the boat. In a seat behind me on the plane home to Nassau, a dad explained to a young boy that they would return home in a week because he had to go back to work. Eager to share my new life, I nearly stuck my head between the seats to announce that I had discovered another way to live, cruising on a boat instead of working behind a desk fifty weeks a year. I wanted to share the dream.

Rolling my suitcase over the sidewalk at the marina in Nassau, I scanned the docks, tranquil in the soft afternoon light. When I spotted Elmo curled up on the dodger, the awning above the companionway, I dropped my suitcase and ran to *Laughing Goat*. Too dignified to slobber over me, Elmo cocked his head, perked up his ears, and wagged his tail as I squeezed him tight.

John left the following day for his trip to New York. While John was away, tourists strolling along the dock snapped photos of Kate shinnying up the mast to the first spreaders, a feat she had perfected, and of Elmo basking in the breeze atop the dodger below her. Kate and I visited the library downtown that resembled a pink-domed wedding cake. We whiled away afternoons at the bookshop and cafe across from the marina and walked Elmo in the neighborhood as skinny brown street mutts called potcakes, snapped at him. I emitted a low growl to run them off that scared Kate instead.

One day, Kate and I visited Blue Lagoon Island for a swim with dolphins, as she would recount in the letter to 2C. On the boat ride over, someone asked Kate at which hotel she was staying. She replied emphatically, "I live on my boat. I'm not a *tourist*!"

Kate hated being mistaken for the pale northerners shopping in town; especially the girls whose sunburnt scalps peeked out from newly braided hair. We joked like locals about their resemblance to the gumbo-limbo trees, referred to as tourist trees for their peeling reddish bark. We were sailors, earning our deep tans on the water.

As the boat chugged along, we leaned over the bow rail, ogling the transparent light blue hues of the water. Kate pointed out coral reefs and shoals that she had spied earlier when she had gone with John on a stingray excursion. When we sailed through the islands, we would have to navigate by eye as the Bahamians did, and I was proud of Kate for navigating so confidently.

We passed a tiny island, and I pointed to a lighthouse that reminded me of the sturdy lighthouses in New England.

Kate said, "I bet if the lighthouse keeper had a kid, she'd be as lonely as me."

Guilt washed over me. I clutched the rail to avoid falling, but Kate was already chattering about something else. I told myself, as John and I often repeated privately, that Kate was getting benefits that were not available in Connecticut. Kate's comment not only touched off worries about finding other kids for her to play with but my turmoil at losing the house and our lives in Fairfield. I was lonely, too.

The next morning during our school time, a French boat pulled in with two children. At the sound of light young voices, we closed the books. Kate raced down the dock to the pool with the children exclaiming in English and French. Their mother and I beamed as each child jumped off the diving board and joyfully counted off in Spanish, a language they had quickly figured out they had in common, at least for numbers. The family had been cruising for a couple of years. The children's mother invited us to lunch on their boat and shared her food storage tricks with me. This was how I had imagined cruising life would be.

When John came home from his trip, Kate and I couldn't wait to tell him about the French family. After Kate went to bed, though, I repeated what she said on the tourist boat about how lonely she was, my voice breaking. John leaned back in the cockpit, smoking. He looked up at the stars and sighed.

"She's just bored. We've been stuck here. She had fun with the French kids. She'll get into it more when we're sailing. Don't make her into little Susie Cole, who lost her dad. She's got us." I filed Kate's loneliness away for the moment and put mine aside, too.

In April, John, Kate, Elmo, and I flew back to the rambling old farmhouse in Vermont that we shared with Pat and her family, for a week's vacation. We bought a share in the house before we left to have a room of our own on land.

When we arrived at the house, I ran into our bedroom. Pat had opened the heating duct, cleaned the room, and covered the bed with the lavender-and-blue handmade quilt we had bought from a quilter down the road. I threw myself on the bed. Children's feet thudded through the other rooms—Kate, and cousins Saron and Lindsey.

In the few moments, before they rushed into the bedroom to check on Kate's toys, I sank into the soft, dry quilt. Light streamed in the windows that faced the sparsely traveled mountain road and lit up the oak dresser that used to be in Kate's room in Fairfield.

During that week, more family and friends joined us: Raegan and her young family, Shae, and Kate's friend Emily and her family. We ate hearty Vermont breakfasts of blueberry pancakes and maple syrup, bought armloads of books at cozy bookstores, skied, worked on jigsaw puzzles, and played charades.

As we regaled everyone with tales of our travels, I imagined myself heading back to the house in Fairfield. On the flight back to Nassau, a feeling of emptiness coursed through me, and I wondered how I could leave people behind who meant so much to me to sail around on a boat. But when I stepped back into the mellow wood cabin on *Laughing Goat* and inhaled the mingled odors of sails, lines, wood, oils, resin, salt, and a tinge of mildew, I was home, too.

We set sail from Nassau for the Exumas, a chain of Bahamian islands in an elongated C-shape about one hundred twenty miles long, strung out like pearls over shallow banks between two bodies of deep water—Tongue of the Ocean on the west and Exuma Sound to the east. Our goal was to reach Georgetown on Great Exuma, the southernmost island in the Exumas, where we heard there would be boats with kids.

As we sailed out of the channel, the clarity of the water disoriented us. In deep New England water, obstacles were invisible to the naked eye, though marked on the charts so mariners could steer around them. In the Bahamas, the water was so clear that the jagged whorls and ridges of coral rising from the bottom, sharp enough to sink the boat, appeared alarmingly close.

Yellow Bank, noted for coral heads, led south from New Providence Island toward the Exumas. In good light with the sun behind us, coral heads were easy to spot: dark shapes in light blue water. However, stationed at the bow as a lookout with Kate, I veered between hysterical mute pointing, issuing warnings every two seconds, and spying dark shapes everywhere.

A typical exchange as Kate and I directed John:

"This way, Dad!" Kate pointed starboard, away from the mass on our left. The boat slowly turned right. To my left, the amorphous shape still lurked.

"More, turn harder!" I gesticulated wildly in a rightward direction. The coral, planted darkly on the left, was near enough that the current could push us into it.

"For Chrissake, the wheel's all the way over," John shouted. He couldn't turn it any further. I imagined the coral slashing the hull and seawater rushing in.

John peered at a puffy cloud hovering above us.

"That cloud is the same shape as the coral." We stared from the cloud to the water on our left and back up again.

"Weird," I said.

Even after we figured out that we had mistaken the

cloud's shadow for coral, I flinched as we crossed over it, expecting to hit something.

Our first stop was Allen Cay, a tiny island famous for Allen's Cay Iguanas, a subspecies of Bahamian Rock Iguanas, which are protected in the Bahamas. In the morning, a picture-perfect sunny day, we motored ashore on the dinghy. As Kate and I stepped onto the empty beach, branches rustled in the scrub behind the palms, and a couple of iguanas scuttled rapidly toward us. Photos in the cruising guides hadn't done them justice. They were huge. Twenty hungry iguanas raced for us. Kate and I scrambled back on the dinghy, throwing bits of lettuce over our shoulders.

We headed to Warderick Wells, an island in the heart of Exuma Cays Land and Sea Park. From the water, Bahamian islands all looked like low-lying green clumps. Warderick Wells was behind a couple of tiny islands, and we could not spot the entrance.

Our anxiety intensified as black clouds scudded toward us, signaling late afternoon thunderstorms. We still could not make out Alligator Cay, supposedly the nearest island. As John and I debated turning around to ride out the storm in deeper water, we spotted a sliver of blue sky between the green clumps, the harbor entrance.

In the harbor, a long beach curved to our right. Purple and orange fan coral swished on the shallow sea bottom, and rainbow-colored parrotfish and angelfish darted in the clear water, which lazily curled over a wide expanse of pure white sand. Away from the beach, the light green water intensified into dark blue in the center of the harbor, indicating deeper water. To our left, black limestone ledges lined a fringe of the beach.

The Park had moorings so boats would not anchor on the fragile reefs. Two large, black dogs romped on the beach. There was only one other sailboat. We practically had a paradise to ourselves.

We headed into shore on the dinghy to check in at the ranger's office. Perched at the bow, Elmo wiggled his rear end high in the air. As we neared the beach, he sat up and barked insistently at the black dogs. They barked back. Still a good distance from shore, he jumped in and swam toward them. The black dogs swam out.

"Go, Elmo, go!" We shouted encouragement as he paddled onward.

The dogs splashed over to where they could stand up, sniffed one another, and dashed down the beach together. We tied the dinghy to a rock, examined a fifty-three-foot skeleton of a sperm whale that had died ingesting a plastic bag, and climbed a narrow walkway through wild beach grass.

Tiny yellow-and-black birds fluttered by, dipping into bowls of water suspended from branches, and butterflies darted across the path. We arrived at the ranger station, a compact two-story wood structure with a porch jutting out into a quiet cove. The ranger's wife sat at a desk piled with paperwork. A baby slept in a playpen alongside her. Rain drummed on the roof as the skies opened for a brief downpour.

We learned that the ranger's dogs were two females who had the run of the island. The little birds were bananaquits who loved sugar-water. The ranger had gone to Georgetown to donate rods and reels he had confiscated from a sport-fishing boat to the local high school. No fishing or even shelling was allowed, and the ranger had nabbed a Floridian reeling in a grouper.

Over the next few days, we explored the beach opposite the anchorage and drift-snorkeled over the reef. Elmo roamed the island with his pals. On the boat, we set out bowls of sugar-water and sprinkled it into our outstretched palms for the bananaquits to sip. Kate swung for hours on her swing and worked on her novel on the computer. I wondered if Kristi, her heroine, had made it to imaginary exotic islands.

To bathe, we used a plastic bag designed to retain the heat of the sun with a shower nozzle attached. John rigged it to the headstay at the bow. He reveled in the water splattering down his naked body while a fresh breeze ruffled over him. He tried to entice us to shower in the open, but Kate and I modestly set up the shower in the privacy of the cockpit with towels for curtains.

One day, we followed a path from the beach toward Boo-Boo Hill, the highest point on the island, where sailors left signs with their boat names. At the top, miles of dark blue, sun-drizzled ocean stretched out to the east. Kate and John scouted out a spot to hang the driftwood sign we had made, a painting of *Laughing Goat*. On the other side of the island, the real *Laughing Goat* gleamed in the harbor.

Another day, the ranger's teenaged son showed us around the island. We hiked over limestone trails, picking our way over holes as water sprayed our feet. We sat in one of the larger cavities. John asked where one would take shelter in a hurricane, and our guide said, "Right here." I imagined winds howling overhead and rain pelting us as we huddled in a limestone hole.

We wanted to linger on Warderick Wells, but it was already June. Hurricane season was upon us, and we did not relish getting stuck in these low-lying islands in a big storm. We hoped to make it further south to Georgetown, where we might find cruising boats with kids, and then sail to the Dominican Republic for better hurricane protection.

Before we had a chance to leave, though, it rained. At night, thunder boomed in the distance over Great Bahama Bank. We peered out from the companionway. Towering arcs of lightning whipped and crackled through the atmosphere before sizzling into the water, casting an orangey-white glow on the black sky. Shipwrecked missionaries were said to haunt the island, and as the wind piped up, a wailing chorus eerily clamored through the din. Kate and Elmo slept in our cabin.

It poured day and night. It was raining too hard to take Elmo to shore, so John walked him up forward to go to the bathroom on deck. We ran the engine to charge up the batteries, but they weren't charging properly, and I fretted about our food rotting. As more squalls passed through, we played cards and Jenga in the stifling cabin or retreated irritably to our private nooks. In Warderick Wells, there wasn't much protection from the relentlessly screeching wind. John wrote in the ship's log, his pen slashing across the page, lamenting the weather and his overly optimistic plans:

Been sitting here now for 24 hours with nothing but thunderstorms and squalls. Currently blowing at 28 knots as another squall passes through. Forecast is for this shit to continue through Friday. Depression setting in. Susan has become fixated on the lack of refrigeration, which is bugging me. At this point, we could run the fucking engine eight hours a day for a week to get that thing cold enough! The wind generator ought to be charging at 20 amps in this weather, and near as I can figure, it isn't.

And if we had left when we should have, we wouldn't be sitting in this isolated paradise with our thumbs up our asses. So here we're going to sit until at least Friday. We're going to kill each other before then.

To continue the ranting...six inches of rain last night. I thought I would try to turn that into a positive and maybe plug the scuppers and fill the water tanks...but NO. The dog's poop is still up on the foredeck, and Susan is worried about contaminants. She's right, but how about cleaning up the shit and cleaning the deck?

Part of the ranting and depression is caused by the sneaking suspicion that we ought to turn around at Staniel Cay and head for Florida before hurricane season really starts. Months ago, with the bravado of the stupid, I figured we'd be either in the Dominican Republic, or we could find a hole here in the Bahamas. The reality is that we will not make it to the DR, that Georgetown has a modestly OK hole, and Warderick is really marginal, maybe OK to 70-100 knots. More importantly, I don't want to put myself, Kate, or Susan in the position of securing the boat, walking inland to hide in some fucking pothole while a hurricane destroys the boat. So, we will, with tails between our legs, hightail it back to Florida and find someplace to hide... There will be a brighter day. Please!

> *Signed, Capt'n John, Master of the Sailing Vessel Laughing Goat*

Eventually, the weather cleared, and we left for Staniel Cay, about twenty miles south. The stormy weather had not run its course yet, though. It wasn't long before thunderclouds loomed ahead. We sailed onward, hoping the clouds would either dissipate or change direction. The wind gusted to twenty-five knots. Grayness closed in and shrunk visibility to a boat length.

"Give me a heading," John called out from the helm. In the nav station below, I checked the chart and poked my head up through the companionway. John's eyes were almost shut as water streamed down his face from the driving rain that sliced through the crack between the dodger shading the companionway and the bimini, an awning covering the cockpit. Kate stayed below.

Laughing Goat raced onward through the murk. After about forty minutes, we emerged on the other side of the rain into clear skies again. The next squall loomed a few miles ahead. We sailed through three more squalls before arriving at Staniel Cay.

That night, we watched a Bulls game on TV at Club Thunderball, a bar-restaurant on a small hill overlooking Thunderball Cave, a snorkeling site of James Bond movie fame. We listened to the bartender's tales of Jimmy Buffett, whose pictures were plastered on the turquoise walls. Buffett crooned "Cheeseburger in Paradise" over the speakers in the background, and the bartender said that he might turn up that evening. Kate cheered for the Bulls. Her last babysitter in Fairfield was an avid fan from Chicago. She groaned as I sang along and readied my napkin for Buffett's autograph.

In Warderick Wells, we had run out of fresh foods, and now we wolfed down fresh-caught grouper and salad. We talked about what we had just done: snorkeled in water so blue and alive with fish and coral that it made our eyes pop, sailed through squalls, and entered shoal-filled Bahamian harbors unscathed. Our table glowed.

Buffett never showed.

Chapter Thirteen
Bravado of the Stupid

Before John left on a business trip to New York, we moved the boat to a marina at nearby Sampson Cay. To surprise Kate, he brought back her cousin Saron to play for a week. We were thrilled to see Saron when she hopped onto the dock from the seaplane.

That night, though, in the muggy June heat, even with screens fastened against the onslaught, minuscule, ferocious mosquitoes invaded the boat. Saron cried as her cheeks swelled with mosquito bites. The next morning, Kate was ready to play by eight o'clock.

"When can I wake her?" Kate asked.

"She's been traveling. Let her sleep."

When Kate couldn't wait any longer, she flung Elmo in the bunk on top of Saron, who was not fond of dogs. With an ear-piercing shriek, Saron burst from the cabin and swatted Kate in the face.

"Both of you cut it out, or I'm throwing you in the water

with the nurse sharks," John yelled.

We had anticipated that Saron's visit would make up for a months-long scarcity of playmates, but Saron refused to play with Kate. I called Pat and complained. She laughed.

"Try charades or something," Pat said. She had three daughters and hooted at the thought of her brother whisking Saron away at great expense and expecting everything to go smoothly.

We snorkeled in Thunderball Cave, a fantastical cavern with an opening at the top through which sunbeams flashed on striped sergeant-majors, orange angelfish, and bright blue tangs, while large groupers and parrotfish lurked in the shadows. When waves lapped against the cave, the fish bounced in unison. As we swam among the fish, a French woman screamed when a big brown shape paddled across her back. Elmo had escaped from the dinghy and followed us into the cave, terrifying the other swimmers.

The girls balked at taking turns on Kate's swing when the boat was at anchor. If we had asked them to write a story about the visit, they each would have called the other a spoiled brat. John noted in the log:

"Wind off the stern quarter...an almost perfect sail... Now, if I don't kill one...or both of the girls, I'll be OK— Understand Bahamas hangs people for capital crimes."

I left the discipline to John, who was annoyed that I wasn't taking a larger role. The girls' fighting didn't bother me much. I imagined Kate and Saron laughing about the trip years later, as John and his sisters did about childhood adventures. At least Kate wasn't bored or lonely that week.

After sailing back to Nassau to deliver Saron to the airport, hurricane season was in full swing. Although we had hoped to sail further south, we were out of time. We would return to Florida and find a protected marina where we could keep the boat.

We left Nassau for an overnight stop in the Berry Islands and an eighty-four-mile run across the Great Bahama Bank. At six knots an hour, we were in for a long day. On the Bank, flat, pale blue water melted into the sky as though it would swallow us up. Without a horizon line, we had no reference point. No birds, fish, or other boats broke the eerie silence. The Great Bahama Bank was noted for shallow water, and we kept a sharp lookout for shoals. We didn't want to get stuck in a no-man's-land.

We kept ourselves busy in the cockpit. I tracked our progress on the chart, John manned the helm, Kate read and painted her nails blue. When an explosion fractured the silence, we screamed and ducked. A torrent of white flakes streamed out of the companionway from the main cabin. Chemical fumes stung my nostrils. I held onto Kate as John raced down the steps.

"It's one hundred degrees in here!" John said.

White powder clung to the cushions and swirled through the air, as though a bomb had detonated. John asked me to shut off the engine and opened the hatches to air it out. We figured out that the engine had overheated and triggered the fire extinguisher, but we didn't know why. John let the engine cool, and we sailed gingerly on.

We were almost at Cat Cay when John throttled down to reduce speed. Nothing happened. He throttled up and down to no avail. When he crawled into the engine compartment to investigate, he noticed a four-inch-wide gap between the shaft and the transmission. The shaft was no longer attached. We stared at each other in disbelief. If the shaft slid into the water, not only would we have no engine and an expensive repair, but also the boat would sink as water rushed in through the hole. I scrambled to the cockpit for a length of line, and John tied the shaft in place.

We limped into the anchorage. After dinner, I went to sleep as John paged through the engine manual, muttering, "We're screwed! Completely screwed!"

A new day dawned. In good light, John saw that a coupling nut was undone. Despite John's pessimistic prediction that no one on tiny Cat Cay would have a large enough wrench to fix it, I found a mechanic who did. John picked him up on the dinghy, and to our relief, he repaired it.

To celebrate, we treated ourselves to a slip at the marina and dinner out. As the sun set over the Atlantic Ocean, John pulled me to him as we watched Kate whiz around the parking lot on her skateboard. The sweet scent of white frangipani, red and purple bougainvillea, and yellow elders perfumed the air, palms swayed in the evening breeze, and fishing boats headed out. John said, "Cheated death again."

Two days later, we eased *Laughing Goat* out of a coral-filled cut to cross the Florida Straits to Fort Lauderdale in flat seas, no wind, and a temperature in the high nineties. As the boat slogged onward in torrid July heat, rivulets of sweat trickled down our bodies.

John passed out ice cubes from the freezer. I pressed mine to the back of my neck. John slid one over Elmo's back to cool him off. After rubbing her shoulders and arms, Kate cupped the remaining ice sliver in her palm.

"This is my ruby, more precious to me than anything."

We doused ourselves with melting cubes over and over on the crossing. The Florida coastline appeared as a long low bump on the horizon. As we neared Fort Lauderdale, a smoky gray haze rose over the high-rises. Fresh from the Exumas, we were aghast at the thick layer of smog blanketing the city.

Kate was already chattering about seeing Emily in Fairfield, where we were heading after we took care of the boat. We entered Fort Lauderdale Harbor, a busy stew of jet skiers, cruise ships, and speedboats. I longed to turn back to the gentle Bahamas. I closed my eyes and pictured the wide curving white sand beach at Warderick Wells.

We left *Laughing Goat* at a boatyard for hurricane season. John would periodically fly down to get her ready for the next leg of the voyage. Although we had agreed before we left that after a year, we might choose not to continue the voyage, neither of us brought it up.

We stayed with Pat until the renters cleared out of our house. At Pat's, Kate finished second grade. After ignoring school while we sailed through the islands, we crammed in lessons at Pat's dining table. Saron and Lindsey were fascinated that Kate didn't have to go to school, begged her to play, and helped quiz her.

We moved back into our house in September. Since we had sold most of the furniture, we rented beds, dressers, and a maroon-and-navy striped couch and chairs for the living room, which now resembled a cruise ship lounge. At least, the walls were familiar: muted dove-gray wallpaper in our bedroom, soft pastels in Kate's room, and blue-and-yellow Mexican tiles in the kitchen. Without our possessions, I felt like we were camping out.

Kate was excited to start third grade at a new school a few blocks up the hill from the house, instead of the older, smaller school where she spent her early school years, though I was attached to the old school. Her new teacher invited Kate and me to tell the class about our trip.

John and Kate drew a large map. Kate painted landmarks: the submarine that almost mowed us down in Norfolk, the marina where we lost the cat in Florida, Boo-Boo Hill on Warderick Wells, and Thunderball Cave in Staniel Cay. Kate told them about Elmo's escape from the dinghy in Thunderball Cave when the French woman thought he was a shark.

The children wondered how Kate fit her toys on the boat. One boy asked how we went to the bathroom, and as Kate looked on in horror, I explained about the long-handled pump we pushed up and down while opening a seacock to let seawater in. Pleased with our talk, I carried the rolled-up map back to the car. When Kate got home, I asked her what the teacher or kids said about it, but she was much more interested in Emily's new best friend. She wanted to knock her out of the running.

While Kate was in school, John and I called clients,

commuted to New York for meetings, and ordered boat parts. After school, we cheered at Kate's soccer games. On Sunday nights, we hired a sitter and went out to dinner, often with Pat and Fred.

Although the house did not quite feel like ours anymore, I fell back readily into life in Fairfield. I volunteered at the fall festival at Kate's school, attended the book club that Janet, Emily's mom, had invited me to join before we left, and tended my garden.

John flew down to Fort Lauderdale every couple of weeks to work on the boat. Cruising books and magazines piled up again on his side of the bed as he planned where to sail next. The Rio Dulce, the river in Guatemala that wound through a narrow gorge in the jungle with lush green canyons, still captivated him. We first read about it when we lived on *Phaedrus.* It wasn't far from the Bay Islands in Honduras. All those years ago, John had begun trying to figure out how to sail from Honduras to Guatemala and inside the Belize Barrier Reef.

Thoughts of staying in Fairfield flitted through my mind like fireflies in the dark, but I didn't raise them with John. I loved sailing in the Bahamas. As much as I longed for Fairfield while we were away, we were not done with cruising yet.

At lunch, John would sit across the table from me at one of our local haunts, and we talked about possible destinations. I lobbied to sail to Georgetown in the Exumas.

"We never made it there. There would be kids, and we still haven't seen so many of the islands in the Bahamas." I missed the beautiful clear water, and the Bahamas was close to the States.

"But we've sailed in the Bahamas. Where's the challenge in that? It's more interesting sailing in the Western Caribbean."

I imagined *Laughing Goat* making her way up the Rio Dulce past monkeys swinging from vines and exotic birds soaring. Sailing to the Rio Dulce would take days as we crossed the Gulf of Mexico and the Western Caribbean. There were few places to stop along the way, compared to where we had sailed before.

John pointed out that, like Georgetown, the Rio Dulce attracted cruising families, and we would find children for Kate. He planned a route so we would not be more than two or three days at sea on any leg. He checked on Cliff's availability to help with the longer passages. He wrote to the Coast Guard for permission to sail to Cuba, a land that intrigued him and offered a stopping point. Eventually, I agreed.

As for our finances, another decision we had to make was whether to sell the house or not. Over the past year, we had retained a realtor to show the house in case we decided to sell, but the renters, professionals who had paid a year's rent ahead of time, greeted her with weird surprises. While we were still in the Bahamas, the realtor faxed us, "A pile of dead rats was on the doorstep this time. I'm going to kill the renters."

Renting the house out for another year didn't feel like an option. We didn't want to deal with renters again. Ridding ourselves of the mortgage expense appealed to us. If we could continue to work sporadically on freelance projects while we were cruising and had no mortgage to pay, we could cruise indefinitely. Reluctantly, we decided to sell right away. While Kate was in school, potential buyers traipsed through the rooms.

As our departure from Fairfield neared, the lump in my throat grew. We gave Kate an early birthday party since we'd be gone in January. One day in the supermarket, I ran into the father of one of Kate's friends, a firefighter in town. He said, "You're living a dream." He suggested that we give a talk at school to inspire the kids and the parents. He meant well, but I resented the reminder of our departure. When I shopped in the supermarket, I pretended that I still lived in Fairfield, and I longed to stay put, like him.

In early October, John flew to Fort Lauderdale to finish

preparing the boat. By the end of October, the house was sold. Hurricane season was almost over. Kate and I packed up to join him. Now, we would truly sail in the deep, further than we ever had.

Chapter Fourteen
Knockdown in the Keys

Kate, Elmo, and I stepped aboard *Laughing Goat*, docked in
a dingy canal in the back of a sprawling Fort Lauderdale
boatyard. Elmo, overjoyed, leaped on John. Still reeling
from leaving our house forever, I pouted.

Sanding dust from John's varnishing crept over the
galley surfaces and the cushions in the main cabin. New
refrigeration parts were scattered in the galley. John, thrilled
to see us, looked puzzled as I brushed my hand across the
dusty pillows on the settee.

"I cleaned up today," he said. "I've been running my
ass off down here. It's not like I've been lazing around eating
bonbons. You were supposed to come a week ago." John
fished around for his pack of cigarettes and lit one.

"It was so hard to leave. The house—" I began to cry.
The house wasn't ours anymore. It would be the country
house of a couple from Manhattan. Instead of my cozy
house, I had landed in a dusty boatyard.

"Why are you fighting?" Kate piped up, for the second or third time. We looked at each other sheepishly. It was John's birthday, and she wanted to celebrate.

"We're not fighting," I said. Kate glanced up skeptically.

"You left me alone to do the packing again," I sniffled. John spread his arms out wide with a goofy grin.

"Family hug!" he said.

I fell into his arms. Kate groaned and joined us. We held onto each other while Elmo jumped against our legs and yelped, eager to claim his share of John's attention.

Later that night, I climbed into our berth, switched on the reading lamp, and grabbed a book from the shelf. Warm light played on the mahogany walls and brass fittings. I rubbed the porcelain pillbox inscribed with Masefield's poem. John came to bed. I was glad to be home.

Cliff and Ross, the friend who had sold us the boat, would join us for the sail to Isla Mujeres, six hundred miles from Fort Lauderdale, that would take at least a week with stops in Key West and Cuba. With four adults, two would be on watch while the others rested. Still, the thought of ripping across the Gulf of Mexico through the night sent chills up my spine.

Our overheating engine befuddled the mechanics and played havoc with the schedule. After several delays and altered flight plans, Cliff and Ross arrived. We returned the rental car and went out for a pre-departure dinner. Cliff told stories of his years captaining a large sailboat in the Caribbean and the Mediterranean. He had to sail in any weather to wherever the owner wanted to be. If Cliff didn't have enough crew, he collected people off the street who needed cash.

"One time, the weather kicked up when we were a few days out. Twenty-foot seas. These guys were terrified. One guy pulled out a knife. He wanted me to turn the boat around to let him off on an island, but it would have been worse in that direction. I had to knock him out. I thought they were going to kill me."

Twenty-foot seas? Cliff wasn't the type to exaggerate. So far, I hadn't been in more than seven-foot seas, which were rocky enough. The next morning, we left, and the engine overheated again. This time, we forswore the mechanics and fixed it ourselves.

It was one hundred eighty miles from Fort Lauderdale to Key West, our first stop. By late afternoon, dark clouds scudded ahead, and it looked like we were in for rain. As I made dinner, I gulped in the fresh air blowing through the open porthole. Rain pelted down, and *Laughing Goat* jolted through the waves, making little headway in confused seas. Night had fallen, and it was pitch dark out. I was tethered to the stove with a canvas strap, which kept me upright.

I heated a stew I had made before we left; potatoes, carrots, onions, garlic, and beef simmered in a sauce of beef stock and beer. When I prepared it at the dock, my stomach rumbled in anticipation of eating it, but now it made me queasy.

Spray shot through the porthole. I would have to shut it, though I hated cutting off the air supply. As the boat jerked around, I braced myself with one hand and clamped the window shut with the other. Every few minutes, Ross poked his head through the companionway hatch and announced how many hours we had until daylight. At first, it made me laugh—twelve more hours of *this*—but as the hours slogged on, the humor wore thin. Whenever John, Cliff, or Ross came below, water streamed down their faces, foul weather jackets, pants, and boots. While on deck, they were harnessed to the binnacle in the cockpit or to a sturdy strap that ran the length of the boat.

We ate quickly in shifts, so someone could stay on deck and keep watch. After dinner, I cleaned up, and Kate wrote a letter at the dining table to a friend. When I finished the dishes, I sat down on the starboard settee, feeling sick, and peered around the cabin for something steady to fixate on. Through the ports, lightning split open the sky while thunder cracked.

Elmo whined in the cockpit. He had to go to the bathroom. John pounded down the deck above us heading forward, Elmo's paws lightly clicking behind him. As the boat heaved up and down in the waves, lightning silhouetted Elmo's curly-haired long-legged brown body suspended over the outdoor mat on the bow where we had taught him to go to the bathroom at sea. When the boat rose, he fell backward, and as the boat thudded back down, he flew up in the air again. I felt bad for him. Kate stared at me curiously, her green magic marker poised over the paper.

"Are you going to throw up?" she asked.

I charged into the head, unable to keep down the dinner I had just eaten, as Kate scribbled. I staggered back to the settee, feeling slightly better. The next moment, books exploded off the shelves on the port side and crashed to the floor. One of the cupboards in the galley smashed open, spewing pans and plates. I thought we had slammed into a reef.

John ducked his head through the hatch and said that a squall had passed through. The high winds had pushed *Laughing Goat* into a knockdown: toppled over on her side, with the mast almost hitting the water. I had read about knockdowns where boats had flipped over and sunk, but he reassured us that we were okay. As he spoke, *Laughing Goat* shuddered upward, righting herself.

My stomach turned to ice. The boat felt like an eggshell. *John said we are okay*, I repeated to myself, glancing over at Kate, trying to write in the maelstrom. John would do everything he could to protect her.

Books and dishes slid along the floor. Each time the boat thumped down, I waited for *Laughing Goat* to slam down on her side again. For the first time on our voyage, the fear that the boat could empty us into the black churning seas pulsed through me. Kate described it in a letter to her friend:

"To Caroline...who is not in a storm near the keys. Mind you, that's a thunder storm-torrential. I happen to be,

or I was an hour ago, in that certain place you are not. Mom just puked in the head (toilet). You can just tell how pleasant things are here. Elmo can't go to the bathroom. I can't play cards or Jinga."

In over twenty years of sailing, I had been frightened before: on a friend's sailboat when the mast split in half and swung menacingly over the deck, or on an ill-fated drunken attempt to tow *Phaedrus* when the tow-boat capsized, throwing John and me into the cold water of Long Island Sound, or on Block Island when *Phaedrus* went aground in the channel and in our zeal to free the boat, John broke his hand on a spinning winch. But none of those occurrences took place in the middle of the night in the stormy Atlantic with our young daughter aboard. The other times, we were near the shore, and in Block Island, we went aground in front of the Coast Guard station. Now, if we tumbled into the water, we were on our own.

Books and dishes slid along the floor. *John said, we are okay*, I repeated to myself over and over, but each time the boat thumped down, I waited for *Laughing Goat* to slam on her side again. I questioned John about why it had happened. Ross was at the helm, and the wind came up so quickly it caught him off guard. They should have taken the sail down or headed off and spilled the wind but had no time.

As *Laughing Goat* sailed steadily along in the still-roaring winds and bumpy seas, my fear ebbed away. The storm washed the air clean, and we had a rollicking sail into Key West. The knockdown receded into memory. To Kate, it had been another adventure, much more interesting than days spent hanging around the boat in Nassau or Fort Lauderdale.

Chapter Fifteen
Mystery in Havana

In Key West, our next stop, John and I strolled onto Duval Street in the heart of downtown into a street scene we had first seen ten years ago. Out of the darkness, a luminous, sparkly man pedaled a glittery silver bike past us. Sprawled on the sidewalk, a drunk with sun-bleached scraggly hair and threadbare shorts asked for money. Tourists lofting Styrofoam cups spilled out of the bars onto the street. Cleavage burst out of skimpy tops. Young women mingled with lean, tanned gray-haired pony-tailed men of indeterminate age. Gay couples kissed. A man walked by with a black eye patch and a large bird on his shoulder. Laughter stuck to the humid air, reeking of beer and marijuana.

On the way to meet Cliff and Ross at a waterfront bar, John was no longer drinking, but we still enjoyed the scene. Kate, though, hated Key West. She couldn't use her swing while the boat was at the dock, unkempt men tried to sell her animals they wove out of palm fronds, and drunks snored on the ground. The place and the people disgusted her. She dismissed the town as a dump and stayed on the boat.

Before we left Miami for the Bahamas, we ran into a family from England who had been cruising for several years. The son, a sullen teenager with long, silky blond hair, didn't respond to our friendly queries. The dad came over and apologized, saying, "We came back before they turned into complete savages." Now, Kate was polite and disdained local drunks, but we were heading into more remote areas. As we left civilization behind, I wondered if Kate would turn into a savage, too.

John and I reached Schooner Wharf, an old bar along the dock where charter boats tied up, pirate flags flying proudly from the rigging. Christmas lights twinkled over the bar entrance and along the ceiling inside. A rangy singer in a blond-gray ponytail twanged out a Jimmy Buffett tune. We spotted Cliff and Ross, already somewhat inebriated, at the bar and made our way through the throng.

"Hey, John, Captain Cliff here says he has to go up the mast tomorrow to check the rigging. You and Susan will have to lift him." Ross was flying home the next day to Michigan. With the delays, he didn't have enough time to continue the trip. He laughed while signaling for a refill. Cliff was somewhat overweight.

"Or maybe *you* should go up. They'll have to hoist you!" Ross was hysterical now, entertaining himself. John was slightly heavier than Cliff.

"Well, I'm sorry you can't stay," John said. "But Elmo will be happy to have his bed back." Ross slept on the main cabin settee, which Elmo considered his own. Whenever Ross came off watch, he displaced Elmo, who whined at him from the floor. All night, Elmo leaped onto Ross, and Ross threw him off.

Ross's casual reference to Cliff as the captain made me uncomfortable. It was *our* boat. Most of the time, John and I sailed on our own, but despite our bravado, still had no desire to sail longer distances overnight by ourselves.

I was sorry to see Ross leave—an old friend, a link to our lives in Connecticut. Tomorrow, we would head out again for the unknown.

We planned a late afternoon departure to arrive in Havana in the morning. About an hour before we were ready to leave, John asked Kate and me to find Elmo. After wandering the streets calling his name, we found him at Schooner Wharf. He and another dog were at the bar, tails wagging. An Ernest Hemingway look-alike fed them pretzels as the guy next to him lowered a cup of beer for the dogs to slurp.

"Elmo, come!" Kate said, exasperated. She was ready to leave Key West behind. Elmo, still licking drops of beer off his snout, trotted alongside us back to the boat.

As we aimed for Cuba through the Florida Straits, the last red glimmer from the sunset vanished into the sea, and darkness cloaked the boat. We were in a following sea, with the waves aimed at the stern. Waves swirled through the blackness from all directions, lifting the stern, then hitting the aft quarter. Moonlight flickered across the undulating black mass like a scene from an apocalypse movie; we were survivors, escaping through a harsh, unforgiving landscape. The ocean swells ran in a different direction from the choppy wind waves, bumping the boat up and down and sideways. The dinghy, attached to the rear davits, banged violently against the boat. After an hour of pounding, John and Cliff lashed the dinghy down firmly before we lost it. After midnight, I retired to my bunk with Kate and Elmo and tried to sleep. The pummeling didn't let up until morning. John portrayed the long night in a letter home:

A twenty-hour trip of looking waaaay up into the darkness into huge mounds of black-gray water against a black sky...heading towards our stern, then lifting it six to twelve feet in the air, twisting the stern to one side and the bow to another, sending the boat sideways into the trough so that the next wave comes and lifts and twists the stern in the opposite direction. The process repeats every 45 seconds or so. Laughing Goat *was a 43-foot, twenty-ton, double-jointed Brahma bull.*

Kate and Susan jammed themselves in the aft cabin bunk with Elmo. Susan kept trying to get some sleep by gripping one handhold and keeping one leg rigidly against the opposite side of the bunk. Off watch, I found that if I lurched my way across the cabin, dove over the wet foul weather gear, lay prone with cushions wedged between myself and the dining table, I could rest, not quite sleep but rest. Eventually…the muscles yield to the motion, and the mind drifts. Until you have to get up to piss, to change watches, or to check whether the boat is sinking.

This is not storm or heavy weather sailing. It is "sloppy" or snotty offshore conditions. I'm not sure if I am cut out for a lot of this offshore stuff.

As John questioned his commitment to offshore sailing, I fended off my usual seasickness. On this trip, I tried a new pill combination that NASA doctors invented for the astronauts. I still felt queasy, but better than with other remedies I had tried.

If I read about a woman who lived on boats and sailed off with her family, I might wonder why she did not consider seasickness an obstacle. By the time I found John and sailing, though, I had become used to my stomach acting as a barometer of my anxieties. On family road trips as a child, I sat next to the window, my head tilting outward. As I gulped for air, my sister would yell, "She's going to be sick," and my dad braked the car while I retched. Through my school years, stomach ailments often kept me home from school. On *Laughing Goat*, I would steel myself when bad weather threatened, take a remedy, and hope for the best.

At dawn, after a sleepless night, we drifted outside Havana. The channel led in through a break in a reef, but it wasn't light enough yet to spot the reef. As the sun rose, we wove our way into the government dock. A Cuban official removed his shoes, smiled, and gestured that he and his partner would like to come aboard.

We weren't sure what to expect. The U.S. restricted travel directly to Cuba, but we had permission to travel there from the U.S. Coast Guard. Still, we didn't know how Cuban officials felt about American travelers. The customs officers wandered through the boat in their stocking feet opening drawers and commenting to each other. They chuckled in Kate's cabin, and I imagined their amazement at the mounds of stuffed animals, board games, videos, and books of the materialistic Americans. One of them held up Kate's jack-in-the-box and lifted his eyebrows inquiringly. He wanted to know how it worked.

They asked for boat papers and passports. We invited them to sit at the dining table and offered juice. They methodically asked questions: Did we have firearms? How long were we visiting? What was Cliff's relationship with us? After close to an hour, the officer whipped out a formal-looking stamp. He elaborately opened each of our passports and, one by one bore down with a satisfying thunk. When he finished the last one, he held it up and winked. It was blank. He had used invisible ink.

The Cubans were making things easier for us when we sailed back to the U.S. Although we had permission to travel to Cuba, U.S. policy specified that we could not spend any money here. Now, there would be no record of the visit in our documents.

The officers asked to speak to John privately on deck. Kate, Cliff, and I looked at each other, wondering what they wanted. John came back a couple of minutes later. They had requested ten dollars, which he found quite reasonable. A few minutes later, two more officials appeared, this time from the agriculture department. They asked if we had any chicken. I held up a plastic bag of chicken pieces from the freezer. They took out a roll of scotch tape and taped the top, informing us that we were not allowed to eat the chicken while we were in Cuba. I wanted to defend the chicken, to tell them that maybe in other countries, there were problems with chicken but not in the U.S. They had already moved on, though. John was leading them up on deck for another private talk. After several more sets of officials had arrived and departed, we were sanctioned to be in Cuba and could leave the boat.

Stepping onto the dock, built on a canal fronting the sea, I looked around at the vast expanse. I had read about the glamorous Cuba of the 1940s and 1950s when celebrities like Marlon Brando and Ernest Hemingway attended lavish parties at the Tropicana Club. Marina Hemingway, where we were now docked, was built at that time to accommodate luxury yachts. It was quiet and well-groomed with tiki huts, low buildings, and pools scattered amid the palms. Immediately behind us, a small battered sailboat from Key West was tied up.

Laura, a blond eleven-year-old, ran over and said, "Your boat is dirty."

She told us she was from Minnesota and lived on a big powerboat across the marina. Laura and her older sister attended the international school in Havana. Kate disappeared below deck to play with Laura while John and I strolled. We peered in a couple of shops along the water. They were empty, except for a few items on otherwise bare shelves. We walked along the dock on the opposite side and spotted Laura's boat, a gleaming white Burger around sixty feet long. A short powerfully built Cuban military officer in crisp khaki climbed the stairs to the upper deck, a rolled document tucked under his arm. Up ahead toward the road were a small supermarket and a couple of nightclubs.

Laura joined us for dinner that night. "Cliff, I can't eat with your duffle bag under the table. Move it, please. And eat with your mouth shut." She kicked the duffle when Cliff didn't immediately respond.

"You like Bill Clinton?" she asked him in disgust, while we discussed politics. She took in the stray coils of greasy black, curly hair that drooped down Cliff's forehead and the catsup on the side of his mouth. "All you ever do is sit around the boat and drink beer," she said.

"I like beer," he said, half-smiling at her. That day, Cliff had inserted a rod into the autopilot steering unit, which had almost burst through its mount from the pounding in the seaway on the sail over. In our short time here, he had also fixed the single sideband radio and accomplished assorted other tasks.

Laura lost interest in torturing Cliff, and she and Kate ran off to play. Later that night, John and I picked our way across the marina to retrieve Kate from Laura's boat. A smattering of streetlamps along the docks of the otherwise dark marina emitted pale, wispy puffs of orange light. In the distance, the purple lights of a nightclub pulsated into the blackness.

Laura's father stood on the bridge deck high above us, one hand planted on the rail, the other holding a cigar as he gazed toward the sea. Floodlights shone on him as though on a bright stage. When he spotted us below, he stabbed his cigar toward the dock in front of us, pointing out a crumpled rag.

"One of my workers left that there. I can replace him tomorrow. They all want to work in the marina because Americans pay in dollars."

He said he was in marketing and real estate. Gesturing grandly with the cigar, he told us how cheap everything was in Cuba: cheap labor, cheap land, cheap meals, everything cheap, cheap, cheap. Americans and Europeans poured in now to make deals as Castro's power waned. The Cuban elites were so eager not to offend these dealmakers that if anything went wrong, they threw their fellow citizens in jail. I thought of the military man we had seen on his boat and wondered what deal they had struck.

The next day, just outside the marina, John, Kate, Cliff, and I approached a group of men with beat-up cars. Laura's father had said they would be eager to earn fifteen dollars to ferry us around the city for the day. The men talked casually while wiping down their hoods and windows, as though they were part of a car-washing club. These clandestine taxi drivers, if caught, could land in prison.

When John asked one of them about driving us downtown, the driver—slender, olive-skinned, in his twenties—flashed a quick smile and ushered us into the car, furtively checking over his shoulder. In the car, he cupped his chin and flicked his fingers forward twice in a gesture that we would come to recognize meant Fidel was watching. On the highway, Fidel's giant bearded likeness glowered from billboards as cars from earlier decades rattled past us— Dodge Darts, Studebakers, Packards, old Chevies and Fords, Russian Ladas.

Expecting blocks of squat, ugly Eastern European apartments of the Cold War era, we wound instead through leafy streets of genteel old houses in Mediterranean shades of rose, yellow, and peach. Some were embassies. Scarlet bougainvillea surged untended out of wrought iron fences, and palm trees waved overhead. But there were few signs of life, and many of the houses sagged.

We arrived at a large city square with a gated park in the center. John, Kate, Cliff, and I climbed out of the car and stared at magnificent, tall gray stone buildings surrounding the park, with intricate sculpted carvings, wrought-iron balconies, and tall windows. Laundry hung from the balconies, and the stone chipped and crumbled, but the majestic buildings reminded us of the city's sophisticated past.

A beret-topped photographer fussed with an old box Polaroid camera he had set up on a tripod on the corner. John, Kate, and I posed as he disappeared under a worn brown velvet curtain behind the camera to take our picture. The curtain fluttered with his movements. After completing his mysterious tasks, he swept out from underneath, holding the picture aloft. We admired the damp black-and-white image while noting that the edges of our photographed bodies were already melting into the park pictured behind us. A soldier motioned us to move along.

The driver parked and walked with us past a statue memorializing the Cuban victory in the Bay of Pigs invasion. People on the street stared at us curiously. We wanted to stop and examine the statue, but patrolling soldiers pushed us onward. The driver quickened his pace, and we followed suit. In a stone arcade with high ceilings and cobbled floors, the stores were empty. Young boys accosted us, offering the best Montevideo cigars, "cheap." Women in tight, low-cut dresses smiled broadly and propositioned John and Cliff. They didn't regard my presence, or Kate's, as a hindrance, and as I wrestled with discomfort, John and Cliff smiled back. We ducked into one of the cafes, where a group of young people talked animatedly, danced to salsa music, and gyrated into the street.

Returning to Marina Hemingway, we drove along the *malecon*, the winding stone seawall of Havana's old harbor, dotted with pairs of entangled lovers. On the other side of the street, elegant buildings leaned towards the sea, their facades decaying with age. Frayed wires hung limply from electricity poles. When we arrived back at the boat, Kate said that she had no desire to go into the city again.

Cuba fascinated John. He photographed the spirited people, the taped-together cars, and the crumbling buildings. Another day, John and I went to lunch at Ambos Mundos, the small hotel where Hemingway lived when he wrote *For Whom the Bell Tolls*. I peered into his spare, neat, preserved room, with papers and pens scattered on the wood desk. We ate lunch on a terrace that overlooked the rooftops of Havana. It was filled with rattan chairs and tables and decorated with fresh-cut flowers. Next to us, a group of Europeans discussed plans to build a resort in the countryside. We could have been in Paris or Barcelona.

The nightclub on the road from the marina blazed with neon every night, and disco music pulsated across the docks until early morning. Cliff, who was single, usually disappeared there. In the mornings, he regaled us with tales of stunning success with women who fought over him. Although some were prostitutes, legal in Cuba, his newfound allure, which eluded him at home, amazed him. He made Cuban friends and attended parties at their homes.

Locals approached John and me as we worked on the boat during the day. One day, I was on the dock struggling to clear a clogged stove burner when a man trotted over with an explanation of a quick fix. With ancient cars and buildings and little access to new parts, the Cubans displayed great ingenuity in repairs of all kinds. A young man in his late teens, separated from his family who had fled to America, asked us if when we left, he could swim out to meet us at the international line. We briefly considered it but, imagining pursuit by the Cuban Navy, we refused.

A storm kept us in Havana for a week more than we had planned and before leaving for Mexico, we needed provisions. In one of the nearly empty marina stores, I gazed doubtfully at the dusty cans of food on display. The clerk dismissed the forlorn shelves and asked what I needed. Later that day, he appeared at the boat with lettuce, tomatoes, bananas, and a loaf of Cuban bread poking out of his bike basket—all obtained on the black market.

When it was time to leave, officials boarded again and asked to see the chicken, which I brandished, the tape unbroken. As we sailed out of the marina, Laura waved goodbye on the dock. I thought about the American and European dealmakers, the old photographer who patiently plied his trade with panache using equipment from the 1950s, the young people who danced in the streets, and the taxi drivers who braved jail to earn a little money. I thought about Havana's faded beauty and how the city teemed with life, partly hidden under the surface, much like the sea that surrounded it.

Chapter Sixteen
Havana to Isla Mujeres, Mexico

We sailed west through the Gulf of Mexico about ten miles from the Cuban coastline, skirting the strong Yucatan Current flowing against us, northeast from the Western Caribbean toward the Atlantic. This would be our longest passage, three hundred twenty-five miles. As night fell, the lights of Cuba glowed in the distance.

Eight-foot waves and twenty-five-knot winds out of the north pushed us along. We were far enough out in the ocean that the waves were steady and rolling, not choppy as they would be in shallower water near shore, yet they hit us uncomfortably on the beam. I put meals together one-handed while holding fast to the handholds in the galley with the other as we clanged up and down the waves—sails snapping, boom banging, shrouds clanking, loose cabinet doors thumping. This was very different from the light winds and flat seas on the way to Nassau when I sautéed steak and we ate chocolate under the stars. By the time I cleaned up, I could barely remember what we ate.

The rain came and went. Kate stayed up for part of John's watch the first night out; Kate and Elmo had become John's watch buddies. As I awoke to join him, John was explaining about the cloud cover to her before she drifted off to sleep below. No moon shone a bright path on the water, nor did stars cascade softly out of the night sky. As we sailed further out, the lights of Cuba disappeared.

John and I stared upwards at the black shape of each wave heading toward us out of the blackness. The wave would blot out the amorphous darkness beyond, suspended for a moment like it was preparing to attack before whooshing under the boat. We would briefly glance at each other and then watch, transfixed, as *Laughing Goat* slid down the back of the wave. Then the next wave would tower up in front of us. Without the blue sky and water as a backdrop, there was no scale, nothing to measure them against. They looked like mountains.

At the top of the wave, one of us would grab the binoculars, stand up and swivel around 360 degrees to look for ships. We had fifteen seconds until the boat began its downward plunge. Once we were in the trough, waves blocked the view. The first time I saw a ship in the distance, I stuttered with excitement and shoved the binoculars over to John to confirm the sighting. He had to wait until the boat took the next wave to sneak a glimpse. Peering through the binoculars, John tried to identify the navigation lights in the few seconds before dropping beneath the wave—red for port, green for starboard, or white, which meant we were seeing the bow or stern. In the rush, it was hard to determine.

"What is it? What is it?" I bounced in the seat as John peered.

"It's a cruise ship."

"What's it doing? What's happening?"

As the waves tumbled underneath us, sprayed droplets, and lifted us up again, we tried to figure it out. A cruise ship, ablaze with light, now shared a square of the Gulf with

Laughing Goat. The ships traveled four or five times faster than *Laughing Goat*. If it was headed in our direction or crossing our path, it would look bigger with each view. When *Laughing Goat* surfed to the top of the wave, we both sprang to our feet, exchanging the binoculars again.

"What do you think?" I asked. We kept staring in the ship's direction while in the trough.

"It might be crossing us. Let's alter course to be safe and aim for the ship's stern." John adjusted the autopilot a couple of degrees.

Twice, we convinced ourselves that the ship was aiming straight for us. Eventually, we believed it was heading south toward the Yucatan Straits, maybe for Cozumel, and was way ahead of us. We came back on course, somewhat embarrassed by our overreaction.

When John went below, though, and I was on watch by myself, a breathless, hysterical refrain would run through my head, "I'm in the middle of the ocean, the middle of the ocean!" I would ignore the solidity of the boat under me, as though I were bobbing directly in the sea and disaster could strike from any direction. I had to force myself to calm down as the boat steadfastly took one wave, then the next, one at a time, up and down, up and down.

For a second, I would imagine myself as Captain Jack Aubrey, the larger-than-life sea captain from Patrick O'Brien's historical novels, lustily steering through North Sea storms. Or Naomi James, the New Zealand sailor who made headlines in 1978, sailing around the world by herself in her twenties. Then the tiniest change—a wind shift, something in the distance I couldn't identify—would set off the hysterical refrain again. I usually didn't last for more than ten minutes before calling John.

John would bound up the companionway stairs and, without a word, my tension eased. Maybe he would squeeze my shoulder, hand me a soft drink to share, or just lay down and doze. His presence slowed my heartbeat, un-hunched my shoulders, and smoothed my forehead.

Once, when we lived on *XL*, a couple who lived on a Rhodes sailboat on our dock in Stamford, Connecticut, invited us on a trip to Martha's Vineyard. After we accepted, John had to go on a business trip. Excited to sail on such a lovely boat, John and I figured out that if we timed it right, John could fly to Block Island and join us there. I set out alone with the couple, whom we did not know well. After we anchored the first night, they started drinking and innocuous comments escalated into a nasty fight. As I watched from the sidelines, the husband, an ex-military man, raced below for his gun, which he waved around in the cockpit, threatening his wife that if she didn't shut up, he'd shoot her. "Shoot me," she cried.

I don't remember if I froze in fear, screamed aloud, or both. Eventually, they fell asleep. By the time we sailed into Block Island the next day, I was ready to disembark and head home. I fell on John and whispered to him what had happened but by then, the couple had made up. John stepped aboard, and we continued the trip. I never sailed without John after that.

On watch on *Laughing Goat,* we followed Cliff's practice of noting our position every half hour, entering latitude, longitude, and compass heading on a lined yellow legal pad. I added my notations to John's and Cliff's as we sailed onward. By the second day, our entries on the yellow pad covered a page.

We also plotted a fix on the half-hour on a large paper chart of the southern Gulf of Mexico from Cuba to the Yucatan. Little penciled Xs advanced across the broad white expanse of the Gulf toward Isla Mujeres. When it was my turn, I plotted a fix slowly and methodically. A slight error could lead us to miss our destination by miles. In the middle of the night on our small vessel, we could envision our path forward.

John had shown me how to use parallels and dividers, centuries-old navigation tools when we lived aboard *Phaedrus*. Like John's foul weather jacket or topsiders, they were an integral part of his sailing gear. Despite the simplicity—the parallels looked like transparent attached rulers, and the dividers like a child's math compass made of brass—they enabled us to approximate where we were. Long after we returned from the voyage, I would picture the nav station tucked next to the companionway on *Laughing Goat*, a light illuminating the chart as we worked to plot a fix while *Laughing Goat* rushed through the black night.

The next day on *Laughing Goat*, we arrived at the Yucatan Channel, a narrow pass of about one hundred thirty miles that stretched between Cabo San Antonio on Cuba's western tip and Mexico's Yucatan coast. It was the entrance into the Western Caribbean where three great bodies of water—the Atlantic to the northeast, the Gulf of Mexico to the northwest, and the Caribbean to the south—converged. All the water from the Caribbean funneled up through the opening, shooting into the Gulf of Mexico and turning northeastward into the Atlantic. If the wind blew from the opposite direction, the current could accelerate to seven knots and slam the boat backward as she tried to head south.

Now, midday on the second day out of Havana, we stared through the binoculars at the water ahead. As we turned south into the Yucatan Channel, the current pouring north slowed us down, but the gigantic breaking seas of our fantasies did not materialize.

We spied the land glow of the Yucatan coast at about three o'clock in the morning, and by five o'clock, we were three miles off the reef north of Isla Mujeres, "Island of Women." *Laughing Goat* drifted while, hearts quietly pounding with the knowledge that we had come this far, we sipped coffee and waited for enough light to see the harbor entrance. The land smelled sweet. Red and green Christmas lights winked from the giant fake Christmas tree atop the municipal building in the town square. We woke Kate up so she could see it, too. The island looked like a series of black mounds against the lighter charcoal gray sky, with a gay twinkling hat.

I remembered our first visit to Isla Mujeres shortly after John and I began living together in our twenties. We had taken a long vacation to travel around Mexico. After a couple of weeks in the interior, we wound up on the coast in Cancun, then a sleepy, undeveloped town with spectacular beaches. We grabbed a ferry from Puerto Juarez, outside of Cancun, to Isla Mujeres.

The ferry did not look promising. Scrapes and gauges pocked the hull. John lightly ran his hand over one of the planks on the side of the hull, and the wood where the planks joined together disintegrated. Mexicans chattered and piled the aisles with sacks of oranges, bulging suitcases, and crates of parts. It was only about eight miles over to the island, and the locals seemed unperturbed. We stepped aboard.

Squeezed in on one of the interior benches arranged in horizontal rows like a movie theater, we looked around. There was not much safety equipment: one dinghy and a smattering of life jackets. A Bugs Bunny cartoon played on a TV set in Spanish. People were unwrapping tortillas, peeling oranges, popping open colas, and bags of chips. As we left the shelter of the harbor, the wide top-heavy boat swayed, fishtailing side to side. I became queasy. Stuffed in the middle of the row with Bugs' high-pitched Spanish quacks in the background, I concentrated on not getting sick as the spicy, tangy smells of my fellow passengers' snacks assaulted me.

When we arrived in Isla Mujeres two hours later, I jumped groggily off the boat onto the wide ferry dock. We snatched our backpacks and wove through the crowd to the quiet sand-packed road lining the beach. A café across the street beckoned us, and over beers, we took in the scene: a sunny street, palm trees lining the beachside, scooters and old cars puttering by, travelers wearing not much more than shorts or bathing suits. Fishermen repaired their nets, and ice cream or juice vendors—smiling, joking, whistling, singing—served customers. We felt immediately at home. John wandered off to find a hotel.

Unlike other parts of Mexico we had visited, where people stared disapprovingly at my shorts or John's long blond hair—or chased us out of a bar shouting "Hippie zippies! Hippie zippies!"—in Isla Mujeres, no one noticed us. Europeans tanned topless on the beaches, and hippie backpackers slept on hammocks strung between the palms on North Beach. Sailboats from all over the world were tied up at the docks or anchored in the harbor.

The fish was fresher than any we had ever tasted. We ordered *pescado frito* every night and licked our fingers clean after sucking each bit of flesh from the bones. Houses were a riot of saturated pinks, yellows, and blues; molded clay pots were arranged on porches; flowers in intricately painted vases spilled over windowsills. John knew enough Spanish to joke with the friendly locals. We visited many times over the years. Even though one of us would get sick for a couple of days each visit, we kept coming back.

Now, as we waited for dawn on *Laughing Goat* outside of the harbor entrance, the gently blinking lights of the town Christmas tree pulling us in, I kept glancing at the shoreline. The charcoal gray sky lightened, and I began to see the outlines of overturned fishing boats on the beach, of pale pastel hotels before the bright sun intensified their colors, of the heads of palm trees looking like a line of happy feather-dusters. As we headed in, my heart hummed with excitement.

Chapter Seventeen
Stuck in Puerto Morelos

As *Laughing Goat* wove through the anchorage after daylight, two boys on a sailboat from California waved. We passed boats with flags from France, New Zealand, Italy, and Canada, vendors setting up wares on an old cement ferry dock, and fishermen sorting catches on the beach. Six days before Christmas, we anchored *Laughing Goat* in Isla Mujeres.

In town, John, Kate, Cliff, and I splashed through rain puddles and knocked into each other on wobbly sea legs. Doorways twinkled with Christmas lights, and the smells of fresh-cut oranges and sizzling chorizos drifted into our path. An empty half-built luxury hotel stood in the same condition as it had when John and I last visited the island before Kate was born.

We moved the boat to a small marina on the outskirts of town, and Cliff flew back to Connecticut. Kate met Bobby and Alan from *Cabaret*, the California sailboat we spotted on the way in, and the children played on the beach.

For Christmas, we strung multi-colored lights up the rigging and our traditional red chili pepper lights inside the main cabin. Kate hung a big "Mary Christmas!" sign, prompting John to tease her about spelling. We called family and friends on Christmas morning; each call an excited babble of sailing stories and Christmas cheer. Afterward, I stood in the phone booth absorbing voices from home while jolly Christmas music piped out of the marina office.

The boaters organized a potluck Christmas dinner. Grizzled men of indeterminate age living on dilapidated boats in the anchorage hovered near the food and heaped their plates. Couples introduced themselves by boat names—*Como No, Wild Goose, Chez Nous*—that we had heard on the radio. We met two beefy guys from Galveston who worked with deep-sea robots and a South African couple who had sailed from Capetown to Brazil. Phil and Sally, Bobby and Alan's parents, had been sailing for two years and were headed to Florida. They had just arrived from the Rio Dulce in Guatemala, where we were headed.

"We couldn't wait to leave the Rio Dulce," Phil said.

Others concurred.

"Raise your dinghy on the davits each night and lock the motor," someone chimed in, "or it won't be there in the morning."

"Don't anchor by yourself in Lago Izabal," said another. "Someone was murdered there this year."

"Be careful if you get any work done. Even the Americans who've moved there will cheat you. They prey on the cruisers."

The dire warnings reminded us of the dockside chatter in Miami before we left for the Bahamas. When pressed, all conceded that the Rio Dulce was breathtakingly beautiful. Still, we went home that night deflated.

I admired how Sally managed the cruising life. She was strict about school: the boys couldn't play until they had finished their lessons in the morning. Kate and I joked that she was like an Army colonel, but we buckled down, too. Sally anchored the cruisers net on the VHF radio—a half-hour each morning when cruisers would introduce themselves upon arrival in the harbor and exchange information. Cruisers had a channel on the radio to talk to each other.

Sally baked fresh bread and dropped off slices at boats on the dock. She even loved sailing at night and took midnight watches. I nodded knowingly when she told me, embarrassed that I had never taken a night watch by myself. I didn't mention that we brought Cliff along on longer passages.

I struggled with homesickness and worried about Kate. I wasn't sure how we fit in with the mix of highly experienced European sailors, impoverished dreamers sailing on a shoestring, and retired Americans who traveled in packs. *Cabaret* was the first boat we had run across with a family similar to ours: parents in mid-career choosing a different way to live. I asked Sally how she did it.

"It takes a lot of effort," she said.

I thought about how rarely I joined group activities in the past. I might have to take a different tack and reach out more.

Kate played daily with Bobby and Alan. For Kate's ninth birthday in January, we strung piñatas under the trees that the children whacked with a broomstick. When candies plummeted into the thick grass, Elmo raced to retrieve them, too.

One day, when I stopped by *Cabaret* to pick up Kate for dinner, the boys shouted out lines of dialogue as they watched a movie.

Bobby said, "We've seen them so many times we know all the lines."

Kate, having memorized her favorites, said, "That's how you know it's a boat kid."

Boat kids: a tribe of dialogue-spouting, mast-climbing children, horsing around with stray dogs at the marina, and making forts out of sticks on a beach. Bobby and Alan operated *Cabaret's* dinghy and, even in rough weather, picked up their parents from town after shopping expeditions; they kept watch when sailing at night. On Isla Mujeres, John taught Kate and me to run the dinghy. Watching Kate operate it herself as the *Cabaret* boys did, filled me with pride.

Cabaret was waiting for a weather window to head north. As successive northerlies pummeled the Yucatan, everyone tuned in to a renowned Canadian weather forecaster on the radio, seeking news of a break in the weather. When *Cabaret* pulled away from the dock some weeks later, I stood waving long after the boat disappeared into the distance. Kate mourned the departure buried in a book.

John said, "Time for us to get moving."

We had joked with Phil and Sally about friends and relatives at home who didn't understand why anyone would leave conventional life behind to sail around on a boat. Phil called it voyaging. John and I liked the open-ended sound of that. We were becoming voyagers, too.

During a break between northerlies, we left for Puerto Morelos, a small town thirty miles south, the beginning of a leisurely trip we envisioned down the coasts of Mexico and Belize to the Rio Dulce in Guatemala, stopping overnight in harbors along the way. Although it was a bright sunny day, rough seas lingered from the last storm and for the first time, Kate was seasick. I mopped her forehead with a cool washcloth and vowed to remind her of it the next time she made fun of my suffering.

As John turned the boat in toward Puerto Morelos, I said, "This doesn't look right."

The lighthouse was a mile off where the chart indicated it should be. We had to cross a reef to enter the harbor and needed to line up the opening with the lighthouse. As the current and waves pushed us, John held the boat in place while we figured out what to do. We slowly inched forward and eventually spotted the opening. In Mexico, like the Bahamas, we wouldn't be able to rely on charts, as we did in the U.S. The charts were not accurate.

We anchored behind the reef in a pretty harbor. We hoped to leave in the morning, but as John recorded in the log a few days later:

It's been blowing like stink...20-25 knots for the last three days, closer to 30 last night... Anchors have held so far. No dragging, which would be truly unpleasant here. One side is the beach, about 200 yards; the other is the back of the reef, 200 yards. Not disastrous but awful to contemplate.

Which, of course, is what I have been fixating on for three days... It is apparent that my naive plans to day-trip down the Mexican coast in 15-knot winds, slicing through the gentle Caribbean waves, were...extraordinarily naive... In two months, I haven't seen one terrific day for heading south...

This means: 1) It's going to be a...long "day-trip" voyage—6 months or 2) It's time to get real and a) be willing to sail in more boisterous conditions than we like, b) sail overnight when we have the window, c) hire some help "Hello, Cliff, John here, still in Isla Mujeres" or d) quit.

D) has looked pretty good during the dark moments of anchor watches... It's been worse but trust me, this is awful.

We explored the town, which had a bookstore, restaurants, an ice cream shop, and a flower-bedecked square. One day, Elmo rolled on a dead octopus on the beach and dashed through a restaurant as people laughed and held their noses. Mostly, John worried, and Kate and I read, exchanging books in town whenever we ran out.

Out of boredom, John became active on the single sideband radio and stayed in touch with boats from Isla Mujeres. Whenever a boat braved the weather and zipped south past Puerto Morelos, his spirits sank. We still had no desire to sail in twenty-five-knot winds and eight-foot seas.

Another week went by. A trip to Vermont to visit

family and friends was coming up, and we had a plane to catch out of Cancun. Before leaving Puerto Morelos, John mentioned to his radio buddies that we were heading back to Isla Mujeres.

We left in the morning, sailing through more turbulent seas than we liked, and arrived in Isla Mujeres that afternoon. On the way in, we learned that one of John's new friends, for no apparent reason, had reported us missing. People hailed us on the radio to ask what had happened. John's opinion of his new friend soured:

Evidently, they had begun calling on VHF a day before we arrived wondering where we are—she really is a Yenta, never met her but here we are, one of her flock. Very annoying. Guess it makes me feel incompetent, that all the boats in Mexico and Belize know we're these scaredy cats who need her to get from one port to another. Worse, as we come in, Mallard, the weather guru, came on the radio to tell us that we were trailing a jib sheet. This is, of course, all from the emotional perspective of turning back, defeated.

In hindsight...things look far more reasonable. The sail broadened my perspective re what is OK to sail in for us— 20-knots, 6-8 seas or even 25-knots. I don't think I have to learn that <u>again</u>.

Our ignominious entry into the harbor mortified John. Everyone in the anchorage chimed in on the radio to comment on our trip, despite John's terse replies. We now belonged to the cruising community whose paths crossed in this harbor, exchanging information and misinformation with equal relish. John's take: we needed to become braver and to move on.

Chapter Eighteen
Bored in Belize

In Vermont, we skied in slushy spring snow and dyed Easter eggs with Emily and her family. We had now been sailing a year and a half. Pat observed that John, Kate, and I sat together, with Elmo glued to John's feet. If one of us got up, the others followed. We moved as a group.

Back on the boat in Isla Mujeres in mid-April, we had a few weeks to wait for Cliff, who was going to help sail the boat down to Belize, a distance of three hundred miles. We moved to a posh marina with a pool and restaurant that offered cheap off-season rates.

To John's horror, our New England reserve was crumbling. I anchored the cruising radio net as Sally had, helped organize potlucks, and at cruisers' gatherings, I performed an "anchor dance" with other women, a free-style stomping and shaking that would have embarrassed me in my previous life. John, the fast-paced man of few words, now held meandering conversations with neighbors.

One night as I mashed avocados for guacamole, I heard a man's easy laugh on the dock and popped my head up. John's laugh that at the start of the voyage was a short sardonic exhale with a New York edge now sounded as gentle and buoyant as the waves on North Beach.

Marring our dockside idyll, John's foot became infected until he could hardly walk. The marina manager called him Laughing Gout. John sought the services of a local physician, who proceeded to torture him, as he recounted in a letter home:

Dr. S. practices in Isla Mujeres. He speaks excellent English; he is charming, cosmopolitan, handsome in a swarthy way, and studied in Merida. He has an excellent reputation among the yachties…

I have never experienced anything like the pain of the next hour. The first local sent a searing hot rod from my heel through my ears. I screamed…SCREAMED…as if they were pulling out my nails…Dr. S. was astride my leg trying to keep it in place…

"OK, I'm going to do a small incision to let the poose out."

"The what?"

"The poose, the poose. From the infection!"

"Ahhhhhhhghghhahsonofabitch"

"I'm confused," he said, staring at my foot. "There is no poose."

It was now time to get up, run and hop a plane to Miami. Dr. S. wanted to…call in a buddy, another doctor whom he said specialized in anesthesia, and who was "next door"… Next door was a bar and restaurant where Dr. S., his cronies, and for that matter me, hung out. I was not happy. Run! Run! Go to Miami!

For the next half hour, Dr. S. and his buddy tortured me with a series of injections around the ankles…When it ended, Dr. Salas said that he really didn't know what was wrong… It took the foot two months to heal.

When Cliff arrived a week later, John still hobbled on

his gauze-wrapped foot.

We sailed out of Isla Mujeres on a sunny, mild day. On the second day out, a large loggerhead turtle surfaced on the water and gazed at us with calm black eyes. Her yellowish-brown shell sparkled in the sunlight. When she dove below the water, Elmo barked at the spot where she had disappeared.

"Where is she going?" Kate asked.

Turtles migrate thousands of miles to mate and lay their eggs on the beach where they were born. We imagined her paddling on her own over the blue miles from Africa or Brazil, an invisible magnetic rope tugging her home.

We sailed close to land to avoid the Belize Barrier Reef about two miles off the shoreline. After dinner, as stars twinkled, Elmo ran to the bow, barking, and we clattered along behind him. Three dolphins dove back and forth underneath the bow, sending phosphorescent greenish-white streaks flashing through the water. The dolphins rose and plunged, keeping up with the boat. Elmo was in a frenzy to join them.

"They're playing with the boat!" Kate cried.

When they swam away, bright frothy trails lingered in the darkness.

I took the midnight-to-four watch. I had promised John that I would take a watch so we wouldn't need to hire Cliff next time. John slept in the cockpit. It was quiet as *Laughing Goat* charged south—just the sounds of the water rushing past and the wind ruffling the sails in a light easterly breeze. A bright full moon hung in the sky, lighting up the water and suspending the stars in a chalky glow. I felt like I could see fifty miles out and a hundred miles up.

Still, I would wake John for a blazing block of lights gliding through the darkness east of us, a cruise ship, or a shooting star firing across the sky. At about two in the morning, John and I shared a cola and a chocolate bar in the cockpit. A few miles east, lights swooped over the water, darting erratically, like flies buzzing.

"What's that?" I asked. "A plane?"

"I don't know. It's not flying like a plane and looks too high to be a ship." John said.

We exchanged the binoculars. Bright white spots circled and dove, then sizzled out. We looked at each other. Military maneuvers? Fireworks? A UFO?

Off the coast of Belize where Garifuna Indians still practiced voodoo, we were the farthest south we had ever sailed on *Laughing Goat*. Stars looked so near that they could have been mast lights on gigantic ghostly boats. The Yucatan and Belize were known for UFO sightings. The dolphins and turtle had opened a crack into another world, and anything seemed possible.

The next morning, we sailed into English Caye channel and crossed the bank to the wide harbor near Belize City. John steered while Cliff and I peered into the distance, trying to match the clumps of mangroves to the land configuration on the chart. Cliff spotted Fort George dock where John would check in with customs, and we anchored.

John ran the dinghy ashore while Cliff, Kate, and I lounged on deck. I set up Kate's swing. A wooden-hulled open boat whizzed by with a group of local fishermen. I lay against a sail bag, glad to lie still after three days of sailing.

From the general direction of the shoreline, a speck bobbed toward us. A man, woman, and two children wearing broad-brimmed sun hats tied under the chin pulled up a dinghy alongside the boat. They were chattering in French.

"Allo! I am Julien. We arrived yesterday."

Julien and Charlotte were from Paris and fluent in English. Their daughter, Natalie, was Kate's age, nine, and their son, Emile, was two years younger. They had a slip at Moho Caye, a tiny island near Belize City with a well-protected harbor where we would stay, too.

We arrived at Moho Caye later that afternoon. The marina had dockage for about ten boats, a laundry, a restaurant, and an office. Anticipating the brutal summer heat and humidity on the Rio Dulce, John switched on the air conditioning and discovered that it didn't work. John and Cliff changed the filter and tested electrical connections, to no avail. An air conditioning mechanic from Belize City pronounced the compressor dead, and we ordered a new one from the States. We would have to wait until it arrived. Cliff flew home.

Julien and Charlotte waited for parts, too. Julien, an architect, and Charlotte, a graphic artist, had abandoned successful careers in Paris and set sail across the Atlantic from Africa several years ago. Julien designed the boat with unusual touches: a wine cellar stocked with fine French wines and a large well at the stern with hoses, pails, and gear to clean fish.

Kate, Natalie, and Emile fashioned a language, a mix of pidgin English, Spanish, and French. Kate barked commands loudly as though she were talking to Elmo, "Natalie, come! Bad girl! Emile, sit!" John and I worried that Julien and Charlotte would be offended on their children's behalf, but they didn't mind.

The kids ran around the island barefoot, turning up slivers of ancient Mayan pottery under the sand. Natalie and Emile would bind Kate up tightly with ropes and run away. She unknotted the ropes while wondering aloud how to say "little brats" in French. Kate led them on tiptoe across a nest of dock lines suspended over the water, listening for splashes as they fell in. Natalie wrote questions in English on index cards and asked us to check them.

One day, an eleven-year-old American girl showed up. She and her family anchored outside the harbor in a catamaran too large to fit in the marina. Her dad, a gregarious trial lawyer from Oregon with little sailing experience, had flown to the Virgin Islands, bought a catamaran, hired a captain, and convinced his wife and daughter to take a year off. He brought along his mother-in-law and his daughter's best friend, to keep his wife and daughter happy.

John and I were at the marina restaurant at dinner when the girls raced up the dock, both talking at once: "The guard tried to shoot us!" They had picked up fallen mangos on the beach across from our boat when the security guard at the marina aimed his rifle at them. "Thieves!" he yelled, as they ran.

We had noticed the guard pointing his gun randomly at boats or erupting in impassioned arguments with himself. When we complained at the office about the incident, the manager explained that the guard's reputation for insanity deterred crime. Even Belize City lowlifes didn't want to tangle with him. After that, the girls stayed in at night.

Still, John found an Indian doctor in Belize City who successfully treated his foot, and I got my hair done at a closet-sized beauty shop where the Creole owner took two hours to color it, strand by strand. When Charlotte suffered an eye infection, though, she didn't want to risk treatment in Belize, and she and the family left for an eye clinic in Miami.

Without much to do, Kate invited a friend of ours from New York and her daughter to visit:

"You can...have a few bonus days and sail beautiful Guatemala with us—we have a guest room. It will be FREE for you to stay with us. Except plane fare. And the whole way, we'll be protected by a reef, so the waves will barely be ripples. Lynn can come, too... The food everywhere is delicious and not expensive. So, whatdoya say?

PLEASE COME WITH LYNN. I'M SOOOOOOOOO BORED!"

Kate signed her letters "Bored in Belize."

John, Kate, Elmo, and I took an inland trip to San Ignacio, a town amid thousands of square miles of jungle near the Guatemalan border. Maya, ex-pats, European backpackers, and eco-tourism guides hobnobbed on San Ignacio's dusty streets. The owner of a saloon, a transplanted Englishman with a cockney accent, told Kate how lucky she was to be sailing around the world. When he asked her how many kids were dreaming of doing that, though, she rolled her eyes and brought her thumb and index finger together in a zero sign.

When we returned to the boat, the compressor had arrived. However, after waiting for weeks, the air conditioning still didn't work. John and I mulled over what to do.

One day, Kate asked, "Why are we here? This is no way to raise a child."

At a loss, I fell silent. Our lives on this tiny island made little sense at the moment. John and I accepted the vagaries of cruising life, but Kate did not.

After tossing and turning all night, I phoned Emily's mom, Janet, in the morning from the marina office and begged her to visit with Emily. Desperate, I even offered to pay. Like the Oregon trial lawyer, we would bring our Fairfield world down to Moho Caye.

Emily's family couldn't make it. When Julien and Charlotte returned from Miami, we decided to forget about the air conditioner and sail with them south to the Rio Dulce. We would feel better on the move again.

Chapter Nineteen
The Belize Barrier Reef

When Julien steered *Little Nemo* out of the slip, the wind and current buffeted the boat from one corner of the small harbor to another. We learned that although French was his native language, he swore in English. When we left the dock later on *Laughing Goat*, a tall Garifuna Indian who worked at the marina leaped aboard to shove the boat away from the pilings as the wind knocked us around, too.

We approached Bluefield Range the next day, an island alongside the Barrier Reef where we would meet *Little Nemo*. A stake marked the entrance between two reefs. We edged in slowly and celebrated our newfound reef passage expertise. Then we reached the next decision point: a turn into a lagoon that, according to the cruising guide, was two hundred yards away.

With nothing around but water and another ambiguous stake, it was hard to judge the distance. The island's low green hills and sandy beach beckoned. John wanted to round the stake, while I wanted to turn ahead of it. John rounded it, and the boat promptly ran aground: as usual, he had not listened to me. We raised the genoa, eased the boat off, and anchored.

I lay on the foredeck afterward, pleased that we had made it and smug that I had been right. We were thousands of miles from where we had begun—no boats, houses, or humans in sight—and we did it on our own.

As I lay in the sun, John fretted about the prediction of a tropical wave coming. We discussed whether to let out more anchor line, put out a second anchor or move to another spot. I would leave the decision to him.

Every so often, I wondered at my disinterest in taking charge. Though I had proven myself at times, like taking over in the storm at Beaufort, John would have liked me to participate more.

It would be years before I understood that taking care of someone else did not mean that I would lose myself. With John, I was building back up something I had lost after my dad died—being able to count on someone I loved. If John were here now, he would say, "Give yourself a break. You did a lot on the boat. I relied on you, too."

John had faith that with all we had experienced on the water, I would know what to do if anything happened to him. I didn't think about it much. With John there, I didn't have to.

We joined *Little Nemo* and sailed to Placencia, a town in southern Belize. The harbor had a broad, deep entrance between large Placencia Caye and the mainland, and teemed with marine life—dolphins, manatees, and as the children discovered, stinging jellyfish whose bites itched terribly.

Julien and Charlotte invited us to sail in tandem to Hunting Caye, the southernmost island in Belize. Hunting Caye had a notoriously tortuous entrance, which we would never have attempted on our own. We jumped at the chance to go with highly experienced sailors.

After a pleasant sail, *Little Nemo* led the way in.

Charlotte sprinted up the mast about twenty feet to the first set of spreaders for a better view of the pass through the reef. I was astonished that mast-climbing might be part of the navigator/first mate's job.

"La-bas! La-bas!" she trilled, pointing out the coral to Julien at the helm.

On the narrow winding path, though, a few moments would elapse after each of *Little Nemo's* turns before we could follow. One time, John needed to know *now* exactly where to go to avoid the coral. Stationed at the bow, I stared in all directions at hard, sharp edges grasping for the hull.

"Where the hell do I turn? What's wrong with you?"

Kate ran up to help.

"There, Dad." She pointed.

Charlotte popped back into view in front of us again, gesturing assuredly from her perch on the mast. Once we were past the reef, we could appreciate the lush, palm-fringed island with its gently curving crescent-shaped beach. There was a dock with a desk at the end—apparently a customs station—two dogs and a couple of fishing boats. A few small cottages dotted the shore.

Little Nemo anchored, and Julien dove from the stern with Natalie and Emile. As they snorkeled in the clear water, Emile's joyful shrieks and Julien's replies—"Oui! Merveilleux!"—drifted across the anchorage. On the steps, Charlotte washed and cut up the fish they had caught earlier.

Meanwhile, on *Laughing Goat*, John, Kate, and I, a less experienced crew, worried about whether the anchor would hold. I was still upset that I had failed John, and he had snapped at me. Unlike the relaxed crew on *Little Nemo*, we had never been in such a remote coral-filled anchorage. We set a second anchor and took anchor watches: four hours on, four hours off.

On the midnight-to-four watch, Elmo curled up beside me on the settee. The deep honey-colored mahogany reflected the muted cabin lights. Every half hour or so, I checked on the position of the boat, sometimes prodded by

Kate vigilantly yelling from her cabin, "Mom, are you up? Go on deck and check the anchor."

Waves broke outside the reef as I circled the deck. The darkness felt absolute—no lights on the island, no moon, and only a few stars twinkling in a cloudy black sky—and it was broken only when distant electrical storms would, for a moment, illuminate the island and *Little Nemo,* the only other boat in the anchorage. As water rushed under the boat and raced out through the reef into the ocean, I shuddered. How little it would take for the current to suck a loose dinghy or a sailor out to sea. I held onto the rail.

I went below, brewed a pot of tea, and nibbled on cookies. My hands cradled the warm mug. Towards the end of my watch, I counted the minutes until I could wake John and go back to sleep.

The next morning over coffee, John was thrilled that the anchors had held in what he considered poor holding ground. I was still offended that he had snapped at me the day before and had to say so.

"Why did you yell at me yesterday? Charlotte has so much more experience than I do. Do you expect me to climb the mast like that?"

"Why not?" He smiled.

I snorted.

He explained that either I had to take the helm or direct the helmsman, which meant that I had to improve my helmsmanship, another boat operation that I usually left to John, or my eyeball navigating. He couldn't do both at the same time.

How come, I wondered? Didn't single-handed sailors have to do both? To live out his dream, couldn't he do most of the scary stuff himself? Finding the way into Hunting Caye was like threading a needle. He was the one who grew up sailing.

Yet, the image of myself standing mute with fear at the bow made me squirm. I had let John down. Kate had been calmer than I was. I took for granted how much I needed him, but he needed me, too.

After my dad died, my mother asked my advice constantly. I gave it as though I were an advice columnist but resented her neediness. I buried my feelings of loss and need for her as I dispensed dating advice. Now, old resentment flared up when John needed me. John and I were in this together, and he was always there for me. He was right: this was something I had to work on.

Charlotte invited us to dinner that night to share their fishing bounty. Aboard *Little Nemo,* she and Julien poured drinks as we sat in the cockpit marveling at the last pale streaks of sunset. Charlotte set out ceviche that she had made from conch they caught that day and served fresh broiled amberjacks with three different marinades.

We savored each bite. Our faces glowed in the soft rosy lights Julien had installed over the cockpit table. We laughed over the ease with which *Little Nemo* had checked out of the country that day: in exchange for a small bottle of rum, the officer stamped their passports at the desk on the end of the dock. Julien and Charlotte told stories of sailboat races in the North Sea and the English Channel. *Little Nemo* was a tiny glimmer of warmth in the vast darkness of the Caribbean Sea.

The next day, we sailed with *Little Nemo* to Ranguana Caye, an even smaller and more remote island on the edge of Belize's Barrier Reef. From the distance, Ranguana Caye looked like a palm tree and a sliver of sand in the middle of nowhere. Nothing else was visible but the dark blue sea stretching thousands of miles to South America.

We followed *Little Nemo* with relative ease through another labyrinthine reef passage and invited the family to dinner to reciprocate for the excellent meal the night before. John and I were below arranging cheese on a platter for dessert when Julien stuck his head through the companionway and asked John to come on deck.

When John started the engine, Kate and I knew something was wrong. John said that the anchor was dragging, Kate's biggest fear. Convinced that the boat was going to crash into the reef, Kate huddled under the covers in our cabin while Natalie held her hand and repeated, "Okay, Kate, it is okay." I stayed with them until I had to run forward to free the chain stuck in the locker as Julien, John, and Charlotte tried to re-anchor the boat.

In the dark, driving rain, they couldn't make out the island or the reef. The only light in the harbor was atop *Little Nemo's* mast. After a couple of unsuccessful tries to get the anchor to hold, we rafted up with *Little Nemo*. Julien was confident that their anchor could hold both boats. By the time we put out extra fenders, the storm had passed.

When I served the cheeses, Charlotte remarked, "I never knew dessert could be so exciting!"

At dawn, we arose to Charlotte's cries, "Ooh-la-la, ooh-la-la!" John and I rushed on deck. In the swell from the storm, the two boats jerked in different directions. The tall masts, each heavily laden with spreaders and shrouds, bobbed maniacally back and forth, nearly smashing together.

John started the engine. Charlotte, smiling, clapped her hands and motioned for Kate and me to toss back the dock lines. *Laughing Goat* pulled away, to everyone's relief. John and I had no desire to try anchoring at Ranguana Caye again. Weaving anxiously back out through the reef, we headed to Placencia. As I brewed coffee, we spied *Little Nemo's* mast and hull against the dark shape of the island, now a pinprick in the boundless blue water.

Chapter Twenty
The Rio Dulce

A few days later, we sailed out of Placencia to the Rio Dulce in a steady drizzle. To enter the Rio Dulce, we would have to cross an uneven and shifting sandbar, six feet deep at low tide that stretched across the harbor. With *Laughing Goat's* six-foot three-inch draft, we wanted to arrive before high tide; if we got stuck, the rising tide would lift us off. We had heard stories of local men in *lanchas* offering to help grounded boats for exorbitant fees.

After an overnight stop, we arrived at the mouth of the Rio Dulce and sailed slowly back and forth to case it out. The yellow-brown water slapped steadily over the hidden sandbar. I missed the clear water of the Bahamas. Only the irregularity of the waves breaking and a few scrub-covered rocks signaled the sandbar's location. We would wait until the morning to cross.

We anchored on the opposite shore of wide Amatique Bay among a smattering of other boats. As night fell, vast tracts of uninhabited marshy land onshore disappeared into oblivion. The anchor lights atop the sailboats' masts wavered like lost stars. *Wild Goose*, a boat we knew from Isla Mujeres, sailed in, and we hailed each other on the radio. Elated to hear familiar voices in this random black scrap of the universe, we exchanged information about the weather and the sandbar.

After dinner, thunderstorms rolled in. Lightning looped through the sky, a sizzling evanescent show of cloud-to-cloud and cloud-to-ground electricity. The crackling web of light mesmerized John, Kate, Elmo, and me as it tumbled northward, illuminating *Wild Goose* and the other boats on its way.

As the tide came in the next morning, sailboats lined up in the bay to enter the river. *Lanchas* circled like vultures; sailboats and jet skis darted about. *Wild Goose* chugged along ahead of us and then stopped. A *lancha* pulled up, and they disappeared into the river.

We approached the sandbar at a crawl, avoiding *Wild Goose's* route. John inched the boat sideways, yelling, "Where's the water?" A smiling woman waved from a sailboat already in the river tacking toward us. Charlotte! *Little Nemo* turned broadside, and Charlotte gestured us forward. *Little Nemo* again showed us the way. Once we crossed, *Little Nemo* headed back up the river.

John checked in with customs and after lunch, we started up the river, too. The busy port gave way to a quiet waterway. Fishermen in homemade wood *cayucos*—canoes carved whole from mahogany trees—paddled by. Birds twittered, and fishnets smacked the water. On the banks, women waded in to wash clothes.

The river narrowed. At El Canon, the sides closed in and rose hundreds of feet, creating a six-mile-long gorge through the jungle. Velvety green vines cascaded over sheer white limestone cliffs like the tangled hair of rain goddesses. The air smelled like rich, wet earth. Herons and red-tailed hawks effortlessly glided on air currents. Monkeys chattered and swung on branches in treetops. Time slowed.

The river widened in El Golfete, home to hundreds of birds, manatees, and other animals. A national park on the shore protected the forest and wildlife. We spotted *Little Nemo* anchored behind an island at the eastern end of the lake and joined them. We did not worry about the anchor holding in the thick river mud, reminiscent of deep New England harbors. We went out with Julien and Charlotte for a fresh crab dinner at a family restaurant onshore.

The next day, we set out for the town of Fronteras, where the marinas were located. A noisy whorl of jet skis, *lanchas,* and tour boats greeted us, and luxurious second homes of wealthy Guatemalans dotted the shoreline, patrolled by armed guards.

We anchored for the night at Susanna's Lagoon, a marina where *Little Nemo* had a slip. We would deal with finding our slip another day. It was enough that we had arrived where we first dreamed of sailing twenty years ago.

The next morning when John and I ferried Elmo ashore to go to the bathroom, Julien expansively stretched out his arm to encompass Susanna's dilapidated docks and worm-eaten wood pilings that wiggled like loose teeth.

"Welcome to this shithole!"

Julien, Charlotte, Natalie, and Emile were eating breakfast in the cockpit. Steam curled from a silver coffeepot, an incongruous touch of civilization. Julien complained about working on the engine in the staggering heat and wondered when the unreliable friend who was flying in from France at Julien's expense would finally appear with a needed part. He fumed that the engine repair would drag on for months. He had been in the Rio Dulce a week and was ready to move on. Charlotte smiled indulgently and rolled her eyes when he turned away.

Later, John, Kate, Elmo, and I ran the dinghy across the river to Mango's, a new marina where I had arranged a slip.

Unlike Susanna's, located behind an island in a lagoon, Mango's was open to breezes crisscrossing the river, and I welcomed the cooler air. The dockmaster, a wiry ponytailed man in his thirties, strolled along the sturdy dock with us. On the way to our slip, we passed his boat, and he lamented, "I never have time to use it."

"Why do you keep it?" I asked.

"It's my ticket out of here."

We had just arrived, but it seemed everyone dreamed of escape. The dockmaster stopped at our slip. A boat was in it.

"They're having some mechanical problems and are staying put," he said.

"How much longer?"

"I don't know. It shouldn't be too long." I hoped he would pressure the owner to leave but instead, he bounded onto the boat and tinkered. He was probably earning extra money working on it.

"But what about the slip?" I shouted to his retreating back. "We had it reserved starting this week. Do you have another one?"

"Sorry, no." Over his shoulder, he said, "Stay in touch."

We were leaving soon for a two-month visit up north for hurricane season. It wasn't safe to keep the boat at anchor. Our prospects that had shone so brightly this morning dimmed. We trudged back to our dinghy, *White Fang*, a nine-foot hard-bottomed inflatable that Kate had named after a wolf she liked. *White Fang* would be our car here, and the river our highway. We sped alongside *cayucos, lanchas,* and *pangas* to Fronteras to pick up *quetzals*, the Guatemalan currency.

We tied up the dinghy at a crude marina under a highway bridge blackened by diesel fumes. A path led to a clearing with a tidy one-room Internet cafe. We peered in. The room had just enough space for a ledge along one side that held a few computers for rent and the owner's desk in the back. We scrabbled past scraggly trees and up a muddy, rocky hill to a partially paved road leading into Fronteras.

Teenagers in military uniforms, powerful rifles slung carelessly on their thin shoulders, patrolled the main street. The civil war ended two years prior, but the U.S. State Department still issued dire warnings about travel in Guatemala. In the Peten province north of the Rio Dulce, a busload of tourists had been robbed—and a few assaulted or worse, murdered. We learned later that the army had not paid soldiers after the war ended nor collected the firearms, creating a pool of well-armed, impoverished ex-military bandits. The young men didn't look friendly. We left town as soon as we got the *quetzals*.

The air on the Rio Dulce in Susanna's Lagoon was so heavy that simply rising from bed in the morning unleashed a torrent of sweat. Imitating the Guatemalans, I slowed to a lethargic walking pace and retreated to shade during the midday heat. John plodded through the endless list of boat repairs. He called boaters who advertised themselves as mechanics or carpenters and visited marine repair shops in town. Everyone he tried to hire was uninterested, greedy, or unqualified.

At night, I ground my teeth and dreamed about the time when we lived on *Phaedrus* in Connecticut and the boatyard botched the deck job. I was still making up comebacks twenty years later. Marine tradespeople on the Rio Dulce had escaped the rat race, the justice system in the States, or hoped to make a fast buck from fellow boaters. They joined a long trail of wily tradesmen who had shafted us.

Kate met a group of kids at Mario's Marina across the river: two boys on *That*, a ramshackle homemade houseboat from Colorado, two girls on a French sailboat, a precocious six-year-old boy who lived on an old trawler and collected snakes and lizards, and Riley on *Big Easy*, a catamaran from New Orleans who was as disenchanted as Kate with the third-world sailing life. Kate and Riley instantly bonded.

John and I watched from the shady verandah as the children played and swam in the pool. We sipped lemonade and gossiped with other boaters about the six-year-old's rough-looking father, much older than the shy, pretty mother, or about the unwashed but winsome boys who ran amok on *That* and didn't do any schoolwork, or the snotty French mother who shooed the *That* boys from her boat because they had ringworm. We imagined that the elusive French father, always away in Central America, was a spy.

One day, Charlotte invited me aboard *Little Nemo* for coffee. Lately, whenever Kate played with Natalie and Emile, Emile pushed the girls and picked fights. Natalie and Emile did not usually play with the group of children at Mario's Marina.

"I have been worrying about the children," she said to the accompaniment of Julien's epithets streaming forth from the engine room.

"You mean Emile's fighting?"

"Emile acts out, it's true, but it's Natalie I'm concerned with. She has been so quiet."

The quietness: I remembered peering into Kate's cabin, wondering whom she was talking to and finding her reading to her stuffed animals seated attentively around her on the bunk.

"I know," I said. "It's hard, not having regular school and a group of kids around."

"Natalie needs that structure."

"Yes, Kate does, too." We sipped our coffee. The sun beat down on the awning shading us as the children played on the edge of the rain forest that stretched for miles. Only the birds calling and Julien cursing broke the silence.

On the Rio Dulce, Kate ran barefoot with other boat kids around the small pool at Mario's Marina and climbed the knobby twisting trees with a blond-haired boy from *That* in pursuit. She had Riley now, too, to commiserate with about their substandard living conditions. I was tempted to paper over worries about the isolation and lack of structure of boat life, but Charlotte's frankness prodded me to consider it.

Before we left on the voyage, Kate was the kid in class who had all the answers, waved her hand in the air insistently, reached out to shy new kids, and invited them over. Now, she could swing for hours from the main halyard, sweeping back and forth from bow to stern—so free and yet so lonely.

As I sat with Charlotte, I imagined sailing across the Panama Canal to the Galapagos. In my reverie, John's new, easy laugh bubbled up, and I wore a sarong. A hazy picture perhaps two years hence emerged of a teenaged Kate, sullenly climbing the mast, wanting to go back to regular school.

As the weeks ticked by on the Rio Dulce, we gave up on our slip at Mango's and moved the boat to a berth at rickety Susanna's. When we walked along the dock, animals rustled in the thick green foliage. Sometimes, gunshots rang out. Only a flimsy railing separated us from the impenetrable jungle.

Now, many years later, I think of us taking a little girl into the lawless interior of Guatemala, so dangerous compared to the tranquil suburbs of Connecticut. If I could ask John about it now, I imagine him taking a drag on a cigarette, blue eyes crinkling. We're in the cockpit of a sailboat, his arm around me, the sun is setting, and he smiles.

"The Rio Dulce was a hell of a lot more interesting than Fairfield. At least, she wasn't bored out of her mind."

Back on *Laughing Goat,* we cleared out the refrigerator and freezer, washed surfaces with vinegar to prevent mold, packed our belongings, and left the Rio Dulce for Guatemala City on a "chicken" bus, a smoke-belching rattletrap peppered with bullet holes. On the bus, we careened through the mountains, traversing narrow switchbacks at breathtaking speed, barely avoiding sheer drops into nothingness. Kate and I sat in the first row clutching each other, while Elmo peered accusingly at us from his jouncing cage in a seat across the aisle. At one point, the driver stopped just inches from a pick-up truck ahead of us on the steep mountain road, and we looked up into the soft eyes of a phalanx of mooing cows jammed in the back of the truck.

At each bend, the conductor grasped the dashboard with one hand and launched himself out the open door, suspending himself over the cliff, trying to spot vehicles coming the other way. The driver never slowed down during these antics. On the contrary, he sped up, driver and conductor both grinning, trying to outdo each other. Every few miles, the driver slammed on the brakes and squealed to a stop to pick up a farmer clutching a mysteriously squirming bag or a woman grunting under a heaping platter of greasy tamales on her head. After the harrowing bus ride, we spent a few days in Antigua, a beautiful old colonial city surrounded by volcanoes, and made our way to Guatemala City to fly home.

Kate wanted to go back to school for fourth grade. By the time we got to Pat's, the school year was underway. To meet the residency requirement, we needed a utility bill.

We had not received a utility bill for a year, but we hadn't moved to a *new* house and school. The red house on the hill in Fairfield was still emotionally ours—the bleeding hearts I'd planted in the back garden, the wild strawberries' light, heady fragrance along the stone wall next to the river, the ratty tire swing. I was certain that the school administration would relent, and I would convince someone in authority to let Kate in. The school in Fairfield was still Kate's school. With each successive phone call, though, it became clear that the administrators did not agree.

I pleaded. I offered to pay. I ended conversations by slamming down the phone, crying.

Salvation arrived when Janet, Emily's mom, invited Kate to stay with them. Kate would attend school as Emily's guest. While Kate stayed at Emily's, John and I would catch up on dental appointments, contact clients, and order boat parts, as we had last year.

During the day, John and I had Pat and Fred's house to ourselves while they were at work. We sat at my sister-in-law's dining table, and in between phone calls, we railed against the stresses, pressures, and high cost of living in the Northeast. I complained about the stifling life in the States: commute to work, come home, eat dinner, watch TV, and go to bed. The irony of denouncing a lifestyle that we once shared while comfortably taking advantage of it at Pat's house entirely escaped us.

In New York, on the way to see clients, I would stop and stand still on the sidewalk as the crowd jostled past and nearly knocked me over. On the train with rushed, grim commuters, I wondered how people could do this every day, how we had done it ourselves.

When Kate returned from Emily's house during that visit, she bubbled over with stories. A boy had tapped annoyingly on her shoulder with a pencil that had bells attached, and she had grabbed the bells off. Her friends thought she should either be a model or a zoologist. She didn't like the zoologist idea.

"No offense, Mom, but they study animals from all over, and moving from place to place is not how I'd want to raise my child." John and I looked at each other. We felt more alienated from our old lives, but Kate was all in.

Soon, it was time to head back to the boat. Our suitcases bulging with boat parts and fourth-grade schoolbooks for another year of dreaded homeschooling, our computer cases piled atop Elmo's cage, we caught a plane to Guatemala. Although we had gained some time for Kate at her old school, we lost something, too: I understood now that Fairfield was no longer our home.

Chapter Twenty-One
Hurricane Mitch

I walked past *Mocha*, the Canadian sailboat with a teenager who would join the Canada Coast Guard because she would never fit into a regular school anymore, past *Como No* from Texas that was struck by lightning on their last Gulf crossing, and past the houseboat of the ragged scrimshaw artist who would ink a replica of *Laughing Goat* onto a crescent of ivory for John's birthday in a few weeks. I swatted back branches and vines that crept over the dock, trying to screen out the hot afternoon sun. Lizards scurried, and butterflies fluttered in the still air. Something—a bird? an iguana?—clicked from the bushes. We were back on the Rio Dulce.

I was picking up Kate at Mario's Marina. The six-year-old boy had asked us at lunch if Kate could play with his collection of lizards and snakes. Usually, she wasn't interested. He didn't join the other kids who ran around the marina, climbing trees in the little park, or swimming in the algae-stained pool. In a raspy voice, with an unusual vocabulary for a six-year-old, tossing out words like "precipitation", he talked to the adults. Almost every time we saw him, he asked if Kate, nine, could play. When we would eventually move along, he would say, "But she was only here for two seconds." Today, Kate had agreed to play.

From the outside, the boat was unremarkable—an older powerboat, forty feet long. I opened the door, and in the half-light sneaking in through curtained portholes, cages of varying sizes covered the table and floor. I sensed the animals' silent watchfulness. The boat smelled dank. Kate and the boy were bent over a snake. I grabbed Kate, and we left.

A week later, John had to go to New York to work on a project for NYNEX. He would be gone for two weeks. Kate was asleep, and we tiptoed across the deck in the early morning to lower the dinghy. It was still dark, with a hint of light in the east. I was taking him to Fronteras.

I handed John the computer case, and he wrapped it in his foul weather jacket for the ride over. The outboard coughed into life, and I untied the dinghy. As we pulled away into the soft darkness, I thought of Kate sleeping and vowed to return quickly. Elmo wasn't much of a guard, but I would only be gone for a half-hour. I had asked Charlotte to keep an eye on the boat.

I didn't want John to go. I never liked it when he traveled for work. I no longer sobbed as I had when we were first together, reliving my dad's abandonment, but before he left, echoes of my old sadness would surface. As the sky lightened on the way to Fronteras, I pouted. Unaware of my downcast expression, I was surprised when John chided me. Still, I had the impulse to beg him not to go.

On the river, we passed fishermen in *cayucos* casting their nets. Flocks of birds rose, silhouetted against the pale dawn light. John reiterated what I would need to do: charge the engine batteries, check the bilges and dock lines, and get hold of Jerome, a carpenter who had agreed to work on the boat.

He worried about leaving us. Kate and I both could operate the dinghy, and I knew how to start the engine, check the bilge pump, and adjust dock lines, but he usually did those things himself. He would have to trust me. I wasn't overly concerned. I was looking forward to proving myself. I just didn't want to be there without him.

From Fronteras, John would hire a launch to take him to a landing strip down the river. A local pilot would fly him to Guatemala City on a two-seater prop plane. We had listened to the pilot, a Vietnam vet, recount war stories from various bar stools. He was reputed to be a good pilot, but whenever we saw him, he was drunk. John's day that began up a river in a rain forest would end in an afternoon meeting in a skyscraper in New York. This fit John's image of himself to a T: the boy who grew up in Northern Rhodesia and Greenwich now sailing in the Guatemalan jungle while doing business in Manhattan.

We arrived at the commercial docks in Fronteras. Fishermen were hauling crates, running, and shouting. A sea of *pangas* angled every which way, attached to or overrunning the docks. We tied the dinghy to a *panga,* and John asked a fisherman to take him to the plane. The fisherman grunted. We thought maybe he didn't understand, but then he nimbly jumped into a *panga* and gestured for John to follow.

I handed John's computer to him. He bent down, kissed me goodbye, and he was off.

I first heard about Hurricane Mitch at dinner with Julien and Charlotte in the thatched-roofed marina restaurant. John had been gone about a week. Eating at the awful marina restaurant, our conversation revolved around fabulous meals we had enjoyed elsewhere, in contrast to the rubbery steak and tasteless bread we now consumed. Kate, Natalie, and Emile played tag under the empty tables. Some boaters focused on a TV at the bar where a weatherman pointed to a cloudy mass drifting around the Western Caribbean.

"A hurricane, but it doesn't look like it is headed our direction. And Category 1 is not bad," Julien said after wandering over to the TV to check it out.

I trusted Julien's judgment. Julien and Charlotte had sailed across the Atlantic and raced in world-class sailing races. I wasn't sure, though, whether he would play it down to keep me from worrying. The pit of my stomach tingled. The others who had listened to the weather milled around, ordering more watery Gallo beer, yawning, and playing cards. A couple of people leafed through the used books, looking for something to read before bed. It was the end of October, late in the season for a hurricane. It didn't feel like a crisis. Still, I wanted John around if something major was happening.

The next morning, I dropped Kate off at Riley's boat, *Big Easy*, and went to Felipe's Internet café in Fronteras to write John and see what information Felipe had about Hurricane Mitch. Before this voyage, I associated the dinghy with New England seafood dinners in Connecticut harbors or Block Island. On summer weekends, we would pass other sailors heading into shore to quaint seaside restaurants—a man running the dinghy, a woman, and children crowded alongside. Since John left, Kate and I had been bombing around the river on *White Fang* together, and on our own. We wondered how we could have been so chicken about it earlier. We were like teenagers who had just gotten our licenses. But we were not on a summer vacation; the dinghy was our lifeline.

Felipe sat before his computer with a small crowd of locals and cruisers around him. He was in his thirties, mustachioed, and six feet tall, an unusual height here. He had lived in the States before returning to his native country.

The satellite picture on Felipe's screen showed a fiery mass covering most of the Western Caribbean. Mitch was huge. Winds had strengthened to Category 5. At two hundred miles per hour, it was the largest and strongest hurricane on record. It had strengthened rapidly from the evening before. A few hundred miles out, its direction was unclear. Mitch seemed to be heading north, meaning it would miss us, but there was talk of evacuation. We gawked at each other.

"I'll keep track of it and broadcast over the radio. Check channel 67 and call me if you want," Felipe said in Spanish, then in English. He printed out a copy of the satellite map and scotch-taped it to the window in his door.

In a daze, I headed for a computer to check email. I would have to handle a Category 5 storm without John. Right now, the sun was out, but that would change soon enough. John and I had weathered a couple of weak hurricanes when we lived in Connecticut on *Phaedrus,* but Hurricane Mitch was on a different scale altogether. This was not the first time John was away during a storm, either. He had been away for the storm in Beaufort, North Carolina. But now, I was in a poor foreign country, in what was shaping up as a major disaster. I became conscious of my shallow breaths. As I sat at a computer to log in, a cold shiver wriggled through my gut.

John had just heard about Mitch—his email had yesterday's date when Mitch was not yet very powerful. He wished he could be with us. Just hearing his words in my head calmed me. I looked around to see people shouting anxiously into Felipe's long-distance phones and frantically typing on keyboards.

Up to that point, our emails had mostly been about my fruitless attempts to snag Jerome, the elusive carpenter we had hired to replace rotten wood in the shower and fix up Kate's cabin. I spent my days tracking him down—calling on the radio, going to the woodshop in Fronteras, and to Mango's Marina, where he was currently working on a boat. I could never find him. John was amused at my complaints since before he left for New York, he'd done the same thing. At this point, though, Hurricane Mitch was threatening, and worries about the work on the boat paled in comparison to my growing concerns about the storm. John wrote:

Got your message. You sound better by a lot. Why is it every time I do this, you find a storm? Looks like it will hit Cancun...you'll only be on the edge... If the wind starts getting much higher than 30-40 just worry that the dinghy is well-secured, you've got extra lines out, and the sail cover has been lashed. If it looks like a lot over 50-60, get the jib and main off, and anything that could blow away lashed down. But I doubt that will happen, you're in an incredibly well-protected lagoon. So, I'm not worrying about you. And if it looks REALLY bad, I assume you'll get the hell out. I do, however, wish I was there.

Talk to you later. Vaya con Dios.

"*Vaya con Dios.*" Go with God. John wasn't a religious person. Was that a joke? The little phrase eased into my psyche as my anxiety rose. Evacuation scenarios rattled through my mind. The only way out of Fronteras was on a "chicken" bus to Guatemala City, usually crowded with villagers bringing produce to city markets. The buses appeared irregularly. I imagined waiting on the road in Fronteras, rain pelting down, Kate and I huddled together in foul weather jackets, Elmo's curly hair flattened and ears drooping. What if a bus didn't even come? Should I try to rent a car? Dire possibilities buzzed like flies and made me lightheaded.

I answered John's email and headed back to the marina in the dinghy. I usually hated the first part of the trip across the river, passing under the highway bridge: the gag-inducing diesel smells, the deafening traffic sounds, the melee of boats in what felt like an enclosed space, and the confused currents that tossed small boats around like banana peels. I would gun the motor and race across, afraid of swamping the dinghy. Today, though, the bridge didn't faze me. I had worse things to worry me.

On a broad open stretch of the river, the sun shone in a

clear sky, but the color was strange, light gray, and flat-looking: a greeting from Mitch, still hundreds of miles out.

As my sense of urgency mounted, all was as usual at Susanna's. People languidly moved around the docks or the boats. True, in this wild little lagoon where tropical heat, rain, and insects had beaten the structures to hell, we could feel reasonably safe during bad weather. Any weather coming in from the Caribbean would travel a long way up the river, wearing itself out before reaching us. A spit of land and a series of tiny mangrove islands kept the lagoon out of the main flow of the river. But I figured the other boaters simply hadn't yet heard the latest. I would pass along what I knew.

I tied the dinghy up at our dock and surveyed the boat. I grabbed loose pails, cushions, and boat brushes from the deck and stashed them below. I lashed the mainsail to the boom, winding a couple of extra lines around it with narrow loops and strong knots, as John had advised. The heavy Dacron mainsail weighed about eighty pounds. If Mitch stayed at full strength, I would have to slide it off the boom, fold it, stuff it into the sail bag, and wrestle it below. Having done it before with John, I knew how difficult it would be with one person. I hoped that Mitch's winds would die down by the time we felt the effects and that tightly lashing the mainsail to the boom would be enough. I took down the awning that shaded the boat from the heat, folded it up, and stowed it. It felt good to take action.

I wished Kate were with me. She would have helped clear the deck and harped on me to ensure that I followed all the precautions John suggested. It made me smile to imagine her worried, determined little face. We would have muddled through together. I could have put an arm around her and assured her that I knew what to do, prompting a skeptical glance. I thought there was still plenty of time to pick her up before the storm. Elmo watched quietly from the cockpit.

I jumped down on the dock to figure out where to tie extra dock lines. The cleats at Susanna's were small wood stubs barely screwed in, fine for normal conditions—no wind—but not for anything stronger. In the States, I could have tied lines to pilings driven deep into the mud. At Susanna's, the loose swaying pilings were not reassuring. I peered more closely at the dock to find an object that would hold and not disintegrate in the slightest breeze.

"It's a bitch, ain't it?" said George, our neighbor across the dock. His sharp Texas twang burst through the soft Spanish of marina workers and guests in the background.

George was in his sixties with a weather-beaten face and gray hair cut military style. He had worked oil rigs out of Galveston, then retired and sailed his old sloop to the Rio Dulce. The boat had a large center cockpit where George and his Guatemalan girlfriend hung out—although girlfriend was not quite the right term. George and a few other oil rig retirees with boats at Susanna's had made arrangements with Guatemalan families. In exchange for money, their teenaged daughters cooked, cleaned, and washed down the boats. Sex was part of the bargain.

I was appalled at these arrangements. The men were old, on the rough side, crude and ugly. In the States, they would be marginal characters on the fringes of society, but here they lived like kings. The girls should have been in school with people their age, not forced to take care of these men. Every Sunday, the families visited, picnicked on the decks of the boats, and received their weekly take. I ranted about it to John, who told me to stay out of it.

When George noticed me crawling around, testing the strength of the feeble dock appendages, he suggested tying the extra lines around the entire dock and jumped down to help. I passed the line to him, and he wound it under his side and passed it back for me to tie the knot. We did that with two more lines. As dilapidated as the docks were, the dock as a whole would have greater strength than one barely attached piece. This was the most extensive conversation I'd had with George since I usually avoided him in distaste, which he had most likely noticed. I was grateful for

George's neighborly aid.

I jogged to the restaurant for lunch. The TV at the bar showed a map of the Bay Islands of Honduras. Mitch had stalled over the tiny island of Guanaja, a center for the shrimping business, and had pounded it at 180 miles an hour for twenty-four hours. One of the boaters, a ham radio operator, reported total devastation. Nothing was left. The weatherman on TV mentioned terrible flooding in other parts of Honduras and Nicaragua, and worst of all, loss of life in the thousands. Boaters crowded around the TV and, aware that we were next, gawked at the destruction.

The good news was that winds had backed down to Category 1, seventy-five to ninety-five miles an hour, but now, Mitch was turning westward—toward us—rather than following a northward path predicted earlier. Mitch was still a gigantic storm. We were not in the strike zone, but we were slated for severe weather. Even in the weatherman's rapid Spanish, the warning was clear: flooding would be horrendous.

The air quality had changed. Whitish-gray clouds filled the sky. In the eerily still air, no birds sang, no animals cried. In a thick gray silence, we waited for Mitch.

Over lunch with Julien and Charlotte, I joked about John's well-timed absence while my heart raced. The marina restaurant and bar, a flimsy three-sided structure open in front on the dock with a torn thatched roof, was an unlikely refuge. The ordinariness of eating another poorly prepared meal—buttering a stale roll, making a wisecrack about the food, Charlotte calling Natalie and Emile to the table—belied my rising panic. My voice trembled. Among the other diners, concern was etched in lines on foreheads or tightly set lips. No one knew what was coming or what would be standing afterward. We could be in the same dreadful predicament as Honduras and Nicaragua.

Mitch edged closer, and people rushed around as the thick gray, silent sky closed in. By late afternoon, the first raindrops fell. I reached *Big Easy* on the radio. Kate and

Riley were playing Monopoly. It was too late to retrieve her. Kate would stay with them overnight.

At dinner in the restaurant that evening with Julien and Charlotte, we ate amid a torrential downpour while dodging leaks in the roof. The dim electric lights flickered. Dense curtains of rain enveloped us. We had gotten used to the incredible humidity and daily rain in Guatemala, but this was different. There was no let-up. The rain relentlessly increased, and the wind built.

I stared into the blackness from our little tropical refuge and wondered how I would get back to the boat. I imagined myself traversing the slippery unlit docks, the sheets of rain flattening me to a crablike crawl. Maybe I should have just stayed on the boat in the first place, although being alone hadn't felt like an option. Now, I was relieved that Kate was on Riley's boat and could have fun with a friend instead of sharing my worries. Stranded without her and John, though, heightened a feeling of isolation in a rundown, forgotten pocket of the world.

Under the low lights, Julien and Charlotte's faces shimmered against the moist darkness as though underwater. To Julien, the torrential rains of Hurricane Mitch were the latest indignity, the last straw inflicted by the Rio Dulce. The friend who was flying the engine part in from France was now grounded due to the weather. Julien was eager to escape the Rio Dulce.

Hunched against the downpour, I picked my way back to the boat in the dark and called Kate on *Big Easy*. She and Riley were playing Monopoly with Riley's family. The girls had been taking breaks to run out on deck into the rain until Riley's mom put a stop to it, fearing they might slip into the deluge. *Big Easy* was anchored in the harbor near Mario's Marina across the river. Riley's parents had probably been as busy preparing the boat and as worried as I was. The ferocity of the storm, though, thrilled Kate and Riley. Most days on the Rio Dulce, the rain came and went uneventfully, almost like a wetter version of the humid air. Hurricane

Mitch electrified the routine.

I woke up the next morning to the same dark, pounding rain. When I peeked out of the companionway, the water was rising. If it covered the docks, it would come in contact with the frayed electrical connection. I would have to unplug the boat's electric cord before the water reached it. That afternoon, I donned my foul weather gear and contemplated jumping onto the slippery dock in rain so heavy I couldn't see more than a foot ahead. George gave me a hand. We each checked our dock lines, unplugged the cords, and ducked back into our boats for shelter.

I tried calling Kate on *Big Easy,* but there was too much static to get through. I imagined Kate worrying about *Big Easy's* anchor dragging, which I was certain she had vociferously communicated to Riley's parents.

By the time I went to bed that night, the water had risen a few inches above the dock. The lines that tied *Laughing Goat* to the submerged docks floated around aimlessly. I slept fitfully. Elmo curled up with me in the damp bunk. I dreamt about the boat knocking around, untethered. It felt strange to be without John and Kate.

The next day, the sun poked through. The docks were about two feet underwater. We heard about mass mudslides in Guatemala, thousands of people homeless, and deaths. The local orphanage pleaded over the radio for blankets, food, and bottled water. Rainwater and mud poured down the mountains into Guatemala's lakes. Lago Izabal, the lake that fed into the Rio Dulce, sent huge swathes of turbulent, muddy water crashing and bellowing down the river toward the Caribbean, carrying the detritus of homes ruined on the mountainsides. Cholera outbreaks were reported. The government declared a state of emergency. The airports closed, which would delay John's return.

The water continued rising under clearing skies. I loosened our lines as *Laughing Goat* ascended aloft, further from the submerged docks. Our boats were safe havens, though, compared to the homes that vanished in mudslides.

The docks were too slippery to walk on, even in foul weather boots. I was curious about the conditions on the river. Julien and Charlotte invited me on an exploratory mission and picked me up in their dinghy. As we neared the edge of Susanna's harbor, where the lagoon opened into the river, we could hear the low roar of madly rushing water. The closer we got to the narrow opening through which the river now poured, the more impossible it became to progress. The water threw us sideways and backward. Huge trees with roots sticking up in the air whooshed by down the river. We turned around and headed back to our boats; the lagoon seemed even smaller and more bedraggled.

The static had cleared up enough on the ship's radio that I could communicate with Kate. Her calls punctuated my day, as she complained about my inability to cross the river to retrieve her. She and Riley had explored the area around *Big Easy* and were bored. They were dying to see the devastation at Susanna's and had little patience for the inconvenience that the storm had caused.

"Mom, where are you?" Kate's voice sputtered with static.

"The river is too high," I shouted into the little microphone. "I can't get through. I'll try later." The channels on the radio were like party lines, and I was sure that everyone listening would think I was abandoning her in this catastrophe.

I had a huge lump in my throat. I wished I could reach through the radio and hold her. I put down the microphone and looked around the cabin where damp towels absorbed drips on the floor amid dog bowls and muddy deck boots. Stale cooking smells mingled with odors of wet cushions. If Kate and John were here, we could be miserable together. I focused on boat tasks: funneling rainwater I had collected into the freshwater tanks and running the engine to charge the batteries. I tried to cross the river again that afternoon without success.

The flooding prevented Elmo from trotting to the

clearing at the edge of our dock and going to the bathroom by himself. Twice a day, I ferried him in the dinghy along the shore of the lagoon to search for a dry spot where he could gain enough footing to relieve himself.

The next morning, I was in the dinghy at the edge of Susanna's harbor deciding whether to venture into the river—was the water calmer or was it my imagination—when a dead pig careened by. I turned back into the harbor, foiled again. Although the storm had officially left our area and headed west, its remnants still clutched us, like the hacking cough that lingers after a bout of nasty flu. The sun was out, but we couldn't get across the river. For the moment, Elmo and I were stuck on *Laughing Goat*.

October 31 arrived. Mario's Marina was throwing a Halloween party with games and prizes. The river was still high and choppy, but larger boats made it across. I hired Susanna's big old launch, normally used to purchase supplies from Fronteras, to take me to the party along with Julien and Charlotte and their children. On the way, we would pick up everyone on *Big Easy,* anchored near Mario's. I would see Kate.

As we headed into the river from Susanna's after being cooped up on our boats, the openness intoxicated us. We wore stunned smiles, like lizards crawling out from under a rock. In costume—Julien and Charlotte's faces etched with black dots, Emile and Natalie dressed as ghosts for the unfamiliar holiday, and me wearing a black wig—we took in the new surroundings. The flooded river had pushed so far up the shore that no walkways or front steps were visible. The shoreline whizzed by, lopsided and unrecognizable.

On *Big Easy,* the setting sun silhouetted Riley's mom. Her hair stuck out in sharp green points like bright emerald ice cream cones. Purple, green, and gold Mardi Gras beads sparkled around everyone's necks.

At first, with the sun in my eyes, I couldn't make Kate out. Then I saw her round face and watchful gaze. I remembered when I would come home from a business trip, and John and Kate would pick me up at the train station in Fairfield. I would climb into the backseat of the car, and Kate would half-turn toward me, glancing sideways as if to say, "You? You left. Now you want to get in my good graces?" The shy glance and little body tightly held together would pierce my heart. I had always hated leaving her.

Now, she was dressed in black, carrying a bag containing a mask she had painted depicting Edvard Munch's "Scream." I squeezed her, crushing the bag between us. She melted into me for a moment as my tears flowed until she said, "Mom, please! My costume!" I let go, her warmth beside me like a tonic.

Kate won for best costume. Mario's restaurant had electricity—they must have been using a generator—and the soft lights glowed on children dashing around, adults talking and drinking. Underneath the joyful murmur, dark muddy water lapped over the docks and onto the restaurant floor, insinuating a touch of reality into the sweetness of the evening as the party flowed on, and we tried to avoid slipping.

Riley spent the night on *Laughing Goat,* and the next morning Kate, Riley, and I toured the lagoon in the dinghy. The contours of the flooded restaurant and bar had shifted. Mesmerized, we drifted nearby. It was too dangerous to tie up at the restaurant's submerged dock. Sharp protrusions might pierce the dinghy or our feet.

I hadn't seen the restaurant since the rain started. Water had risen to the tops of the bar stools. The bartender sloshed around the back of the bar in water up to his chest, serving drinks to two grizzled old men, probably my neighbor George's cohorts. As I gazed at the silent drinking men, I imagined them riding out the hurricane there, through the deluge that overwhelmed three countries. Warm dirty water would have reached their waists as they sat unperturbed, and the bartender attentively refilled their smudged glasses.

Busy with boat tasks later that morning, I poked my head out to check on the girls.

"Here! It's over here!" Kate shrieked from the water, waving to Riley.

They were establishing finish lines for a swim race between our dock—now three feet underwater—and the dock across from us. They howled with laughter at their inability to see the docks in the murky water. A foot-long bright chartreuse slug slithered toward them, its pop-eyed, whiskered head swiveling back and forth above the surface. Mitch had churned up this ancient beast from the deep. I pointed to the hideous animal and screamed at them to get out of the water.

The slug, though, fascinated them. As I conjured up other possibilities—catching cholera, cutting themselves on the underwater dock—they ignored me. Free for the first time in days, they weren't about to give in. Eventually, they climbed back on the boat and rinsed off with fresh water. At least, the girls had enjoyed the swollen river that had imperiled so many. Julien stopped by and told me that he had called his mother in France in the office upstairs from the marina restaurant. After lunch, I ran the dinghy over to the restaurant to call John. I tied up at the broken submerged dock and picked my way to the now empty bar.

Weighed down by a foul weather jacket and overalls, I slogged through the dark restaurant in water up to my waist. The heavy mahogany furniture, overturned and floating, was invisible in the gloom until I thumped into it. My boots filled with water. It was insufferably hot and smelled like rotting food. Dripping sweat blinded me. I slid in the muck and banged into a sunken chair. I worried that I might twist an ankle or break an arm, and no one would know.

I carefully mounted the slick muddy steps to the office, lowered myself onto a chair, and unzipped my jacket to cool off. I expected the phone to be dead but there was a dial tone. John had finished his project and was now staying at Pat's, waiting for the Guatemala City airport to open so he could return home. I tried the operator. The phone rang and then stopped. I tried again and again. Sometimes, I heard an incomprehensible message in Spanish before the phone died. I couldn't get through.

I headed across the river to Felipe's Internet cafe on a choppy wet ride I had hoped to avoid, and I reached John on Felipe's phone. I don't remember the short conversation, but hearing his voice, my body shook. I leaned against a wall. My shoulders, which must have been scrunched up to my ears, relaxed. The government had just announced the re-opening of Guatemala City's airport, and John would be on the first plane out of New York the next day.

I wrote to relatives and friends about the storm to let them know we were okay, although I wasn't sure that they even knew we were in danger: *I'll bet you're wondering about Kate and me during all the weather. It was quite an adventure...*

I didn't reach my swashbuckling literary hero Captain Jack Aubrey's heights of bravery, but I was proud of myself. I had never faced a situation of this magnitude while apart from John. Before our voyage, I would not have imagined myself charging across the river on the dinghy or handling a boat in a hurricane. Sitting in front of the computer at Felipe's shop now that the worst was over, I read the emails from John that I hadn't been able to cross the river to retrieve earlier.

...Have my last emails got you so pissed off or depressed that you can't bear the thought of writing me? I love you. It's no great shakes up here either...Kate, I miss you very, very much...your cute little smile, seeing you there asleep on the floor, the frown on your face, all of you. Write me, you awful child...

It's driving me nuts that I'm not there with you. On the one hand, the current info is that the worst will pass you by, and I should not worry... Nice cozy lagoon, well-protected, etc.... On the other hand, my mind is going through the same worry list that I'm sure your mind is going through, but I can't do anything about it, I can only imagine scenes and mentally tell you what to do...which, of course, doesn't help...

I love you very much and am truly sorry I'm not there for you. Oh, just a second, they've just brought up some fresh raspberries...

In his last email before Mitch arrived, he said, "Finally, sweetheart, if things look like they're going to get out of hand, do not hesitate to go to Guatemala City. Just secure the boat as best you can and get out."

I love reading the emails now, twenty years later. Protect the boat but don't be a fool. "Sweetheart" sounds nice, too. We didn't use terms of endearment much. In my twenties, I denounced them as an objectification of women. Much later, though, John called me sweetheart and honey, sometimes when he was trying to get through to me about something I resisted, and I liked it.

In a photo I have of the bar at Susanna's Lagoon about a week after the storm, the water level has dropped to only a few inches above the floor. A greenish-brown waterline rims the bamboo wall under the mahogany bar. The two old men sit on their stools at the back of the bar squinting out at the sun, Gallo beers plunked in front of them. The smiling bartender sets out a Coke with a glass of ice along the front side of the bar for someone else. I imagine sipping the Coke, the red vinyl barstool still damp, my knees knocking against the muddy stained bamboo, and the entire bar—the entire coastline—reeking of mildew. Estimates were that Mitch left 11,000 dead, mostly in Honduras and Nicaragua, and many more thousands throughout Central America homeless.

Two days later, after a delay in Guatemala City when John's plane from New York couldn't land because of all the humanitarian flights, a small prop plane circled Susanna's Lagoon and dipped its wing. The pilot had brought John home.

A *panga* delivered John to the boat. Elmo spotted him

first and leaped up, yipping. John peered at the water, still two feet above the docks, with the same slack-jawed expression that we all had when we first encountered post-Mitch reality. He tossed his duffel and computer on deck and hoisted himself up. We held each other for a long time.

He said, "On the flight here, all I saw was mud, like the whole country was washed away. You were brave."

Kate and I regaled him with Mitch stories.

Chapter Twenty-Two
Land of Rules

Hurricane season officially ended. Julien's friend arrived with the wrong engine part. When we walked past *Little Nemo*, we could hear Julien grumbling from the engine room.

Big Easy left. The last time Riley's mom drew up the dinghy to fetch Riley, she refused to come out of Kate's cabin. Through the hatch, she yelled to her mom that she didn't want to sail to Panama and was sick of sailing with her parents. *Big Easy* was heading through the Panama Canal to California to sell the boat, their year of cruising at an end. They were moving back to New Orleans.

Jerome, the carpenter, started work on *Laughing Goat*. On the first day, he arrived wordlessly on his dinghy with a large green parrot on his shoulder. He gracefully unfolded a tall, lanky frame, nodded hello, and proceeded to bang on the floorboards in the head. He was an introverted artist, extraordinarily skillful with wood. At the end of the day, he asked us to move off the boat; our presence disturbed him. We were taken aback but to avoid resentment, we stayed at a hacienda on a rubber plantation across the river from the marina.

The hacienda's grounds resembled an enchanted forest, with masses of flowering bushes and rope bridges swinging over bubbling streams. We stayed in a rambling two-story wood palapa with carved mahogany chests and canopy beds draped with gauzy white mosquito nets. Sun streamed in from tall wood-framed windows.

We invented pretexts to stop by the boat. Now that we were out of his hair, Jerome was friendly, but if we stayed too long, he turned his back and pounded wood. When he finished, we had a beautiful teak bench and handrails in the shower, and Kate had an elegant new headboard with two leaping dolphins.

Next, we hauled *Laughing Goat* out of the water at a tiny boatyard up the river. While the boatyard workers worked on the boat's bottom, we took a trip to Antigua, a favorite, and Guatemala City. We left Elmo with Julien on *Little Nemo*.

When we returned, Julien was even more foul-tempered than usual. During a storm, Elmo had whined under the dining table and disrupted Julien's sleep. We proffered French cheeses from a gourmet shop in Guatemala City, but our relationship deteriorated. When we went out to lunch one day on Lago Izabal, Emile rammed *White Fang* with *Little Nemo's* dinghy. John and I were not amused. Julien and Charlotte began socializing exclusively with French-speaking cruisers.

Little Nemo eventually set out for the Bay Islands in Honduras. They planned to cross the Pacific to the South Seas. We inquired about them on the cruisers' radio net and learned they had made it safely to Panama. I imagined them cruising onward, Julien irascible, Natalie quiet, Emile antisocial, and Charlotte holding it all together.

The precocious six-year-old and his parents left, too, bound for Florida. A week later, the FBI called the owner of Mario's Marina. The marine police in Florida had received a radio call from the boat while underway. The boy's mother had fallen overboard and drowned. His stepfather said that she was drunk. The boy and his stepfather towed her body to Key West in the dinghy. Rumors flew that the stepfather had been the mother's parole officer who regularly beat her. I wondered how the boy would overcome such a ghastly event.

The remaining cruisers celebrated Thanksgiving dinner at a restaurant on the water. More boats left the Rio Dulce, and pressure mounted for us to move along, too. We wanted to spend Christmas in Isla Mujeres but had not yet resolved what to do after that. We decided to postpone the decision about our future until after a ski trip in February with Pat and the cousins in Vermont.

Cliff flew down to help us sail back to Isla Mujeres. The night before we left the Rio Dulce, we filled the tanks at the Esso station with its 1950's red and white relic sign. John and Kate had often puttered on the dinghy after dinner to the Esso gas dock. The soft rumbling of the outboard would carry down the river, and while I finished up the dishes, I could just make out three figures fading into the velvet brown dusk with Elmo perched at the bow. They would return with stale, crumbly American chocolate bars— a taste of home. The last night, they bought a pile for the trip.

In the morning, we bid farewell to Susanna's Lagoon. I glanced at Fronteras' harbor as we sailed by and pictured evening twilight when the round leafy trees teemed with hundreds of egrets flying about in a deafening rush of beating wings and eerie shrieks. In the early morning sun, though, the trees stood silent and still.

We passed Mario's Marina. *That* was still there. We heard a few months later that the grandparents descended from Colorado to enroll the younger boys in school. The two girls on the French boat waved.

The river opened up at El Golfete into a broad, cool expanse. After so much time bottled up on the river, the sight of the opening exhilarated us. Kate climbed up the forestay.

Elmo joined her at the bow. Fishermen in *cayucos* slowly traversed the bay, casting nets. We rounded the bend and came upon El Canon. The steep jungle canyon sides plunged toward us, almost close enough to touch. Red-tailed hawks drifted on upper air currents, flowered vines dripped from the tree canopy, and the wind rustled through the shiny green leaves. The raw beauty of El Canon again left us agape, overcome at the privilege of passing through such a setting.

We neared the mouth of the river and inhaled the briny sea air. We tied up at the dock in Livingston, and John checked us out of Guatemala. I lay down in the cockpit with a book, breathing in the fresh scent of the open sea. I didn't want to move.

After stops in Placencia and Belize City, we sailed out of English Caye harbor with a forecast of northeast winds and ten-foot seas from a cold front coming south. We sailed along the coastline in the protection of the Belize Barrier Reef. Not thinking about it too much, I slapped on a wristband recommended by deep-sea fishermen for motion sickness, instead of taking my usual strong medications.

John noted December 21:

Seas were moderate, a slow succession of swells with smaller waves on top. We are all in a good mood, though Cliff is...concerned about making Isla before the cold front comes too far south. Winds behind it are about 40-50 knots.

Susan...made us all scrambled eggs and stuff as we were coming out of English Caye channel. Was the last meal she'd be able to cook.

I noticed that she was wearing a wristband with a white dot. Recommended by a pharmacist, she said, it's what all the fishermen swear by. Cool, I thought. No pills.

By late afternoon, we were emerging out from the shadow of the...reef, which provides a fair amount of protection from NE-SE wind and swells that have been marching across the Atlantic driven by the easterly trades. Wind increased to 15-20, whitecaps on the wind waves.

Susan is now very sick. She tried taking her pills, but

they have not kicked in. Seas are up to 8'. They appear 16'
from the trough, but the boat doesn't really notice them. Just
rises to meet each one and then heads down its face. The
movement below is...awkward...like moving around in a
bucking jungle gym.

Utterly miserable, I lay in my bunk, gaining relief only
after a bout of nausea. I braced my foot, but my body still
banged against the bunk while the boat careened up and
down. After my stomach emptied, dry heaves started. I
wanted to throw myself off the boat or die. As evening fell,
I lay in the muggy darkness of the cabin, seeing no end to
the torment.

Kate checked on me periodically. Her light breath
warmed my cheek, and my eyes would open under her eager
gaze. She scrutinized my face as though I were a lab
specimen and shouted reports to John in the cockpit: "Hey,
Dad, she's turning green! Come look!" The engine droned
on relentlessly, and diesel fumes oozed in. I vowed to myself
that if I lived through the night, I would never sail again.

The night stretched on. At one point, John hurled a
bundle of wet fur onto the bunk with me: Elmo, drenched
from rain and sea spray. My partner in seasickness was
under the weather, too. He curled up in a corner, his hair
dripping. After staying up with John on watch, Kate crawled
in with Elmo and me. She asked why I clutched a towel.

"Just in case," I said. She sprinted out of the berth.

Then the engine stopped. No more fumes, no more
droning noise.

"What's going on?" I asked Cliff, who was in the
engine room.

"There's water in the fuel. We have to drain the lines
and switch tanks." He sounded tired and irritable.

We had filled the tanks at the Esso station on the Rio
Dulce. Water must have seeped into the Esso supply after
the hurricane. I was glad that Cliff was here, and that John
didn't have to deal with the problem alone in the middle of
the night. John, steering the boat, yelled something to Cliff

about Cayo Norte, a reef near the Mexican coast. He wanted to know how much longer Cliff thought it would take; we were closing in on the reef, and without the engine, we didn't have steerageway. I fell asleep to tense exchanges between John and Cliff as *Laughing Goat* tacked between Cayo Norte and the shore. John's version:

Kate's fine, pops her head up once in a while but then goes back to reading. The dog is like Susan...miserable. He keeps trying to climb up my armpit for safety.

Night was coming... Switched fuel tanks. Engine died. Water filled the Racor (filter). Drained the Racor, changed...filters, bled the system, and eventually, the engine restarted. While Cliff was earning his considerable salary doing this... Wind died to less than 15. Kate was unhappy—as she is anytime we are apparently floating and out of control.

I kept checking the position, as the lights of Xcaret were getting larger and larger. We...were being pushed toward the reef... Ran out of fuel 8:00 am. Cliff and I emptied the water from the bad tank...when we got to good fuel, bled the system, and off we went.

Wind and seas building... Susan still sick.

I'm tired but OK. My thoughts have evolved from the "how can I do this to myself and wife and child, if something happened, we'd all drown" —which are my usual thoughts first day out...offshore—to continual amazement at how the boat moves and...easily rises and falls in the sea, and I...instinctively understand how she could...handle much more.

Also, since these are the largest waves we've been in, I began to understand that size is not that big a deal, to a point...these could be 15', and the boat would be as comfortable...as long as the wave shape remained rounded. It's when they stand up and get short and steep that we get beat up...

And I remembered the dolphin...20' from me as I sat at the wheel, he shot out of the back of a wave that had just

passed—in mid-flight to then dive under the boat.
  On we go.
  On we go.

I felt slightly better in the morning and joined everyone in the cockpit. Cliff and John had little sleep, and we decided to rest in Cozumel. As soon as we entered Cozumel harbor, the motion blessedly ceased. I became positively chipper. I heated chili for dinner, and everyone enjoyed a good night's sleep.

Overnight, the wind shifted. The next day, *Laughing Goat* charged to Isla Mujeres through boisterous seas. With the wind now on the beam, the boat's jerky motion eased. I stayed on deck in the fresh air.

Along the Mexican coast, sunbathers freckled the beach. A familiar hump materialized on the horizon, and the triangular shape of the town Christmas tree that overlooked the central plaza in Isla Mujeres came into focus as it had one year ago.

Over the Christmas holiday, friends visited from the States. Kate met an Italian girl, also nine, who had sailed to Mexico with her dad from Virginia. While the girl enthusiastically recounted adventures with her father—she cooked meals, steered the boat, and kept watch by herself—Kate stared at her in disbelief. *Até*, a boat we had run across on the Rio Dulce turned up, too. Juliet, a teacher, and Mark, an engineer, had sailed over from England with their daughter, Bonnie, who was Kate's age, and son Rory, six; they were on their way to a new home in Hong Kong.

One time, Kate was playing a word game on *Até* and guessed "pants," in response to a drawing of long pants, while Bonnie and Rory held out for "trousers." Kate accused them of cheating. They were just as certain that "trousers" was correct. While the adults found the cultural difference amusing, Kate did not.

For Kate's tenth birthday in January, we invited Bonnie

and Rory to Wet n' Wild, a water park in Cancun. Bonnie and Rory had a great time, but Kate wound up crying into her birthday cake. She missed her partner in crime, Riley, who shared her sardonic view of life. She missed the easy companionship of Bobby and Alan, with whom she had gone to Wet n' Wild the year before.

We capped off the day with a birthday dinner for the three of us at a favorite restaurant on the island. While mariachi singers in outsized sombreros gaily serenaded Kate, she cried. She wrote to a friend: *I went to a place called Wet n' Wild. Everyone thought I was Mexican and started speaking Spanish to me. They should stop doing it.*

Although John and I had decided to wait until after the February trip to decide what we were going to do next, one morning over coffee in the cockpit, John asked, "What if we could find a way to keep cruising while we put Kate in school?"

I looked at John over the rim of my cup. Was he thinking of boarding school?

"What if we went back to Fairfield? Maybe we could keep the boat somewhere down in Florida or even here on Isla, and sail for a few months of the year," I said.

Once I said it, it dawned on me how much I still hoped that we could slip into our old lives. John was quiet, smoking, gazing at the fishing boats heading in.

"I can't do it," he said. "I can't go back to New York. I'd have to compete with all the yuppie assholes again."

John recently made money on the stock market and hoped that we wouldn't have to work at all, or only occasionally, if we moved somewhere with a lower cost of living, ruling out Fairfield. I tried again.

"How about Florida? It's warm. We could find somewhere with good schools. It would be someplace we could sail out of." Florida, the jumping-off point for the voyage, had just popped out.

"It sounds like death," John replied, probably envisioning doddering oldsters brandishing their walkers.

As I thought about it, I had to agree.

We flew to Connecticut for the February vacation. Kate joined Emily at school for a few days while John and I stayed with Pat and Fred. We skied for a week in Vermont with relatives and friends. The visit buoyed all of us.

We returned to Isla Mujeres with the same conundrum awaiting us. In our heads swirled *Laughing Goat* gliding through the jungle in El Canon, anchored in the transparent water of Warderick Wells or flying through a star-filled night in Belize while dolphins played at the bow. What lay ahead we didn't yet know.

John and I stumbled through fitful discussions about the future while Kate and I struggled with fourth-grade lessons. One day, she and I sat at the table in the main cabin, with notebooks, pencils, and textbooks scattered over the surface.

"What's six times six?" I asked. She looked at me appraisingly.

"What's that on your face, those red bumps?" She leaned in for a closer examination.

"C'mon, Kate, six times six."

"No, really, it looks like a rash or something."

Various skin eruptions, locally known as jungle rot, afflicted us in the tropics. John and Kate spent hours exclaiming over pictures of disgusting tropical skin diseases and insect bites.

Kate continued, "I think the thing on your face is moving."

"Kate, you have to do the times tables."

"I hate them."

"You'll never do well in math until you know these. Let's try four times four." Kate drew on a piece of paper, concentrating on her moving pencil. I shot up, bumping my legs against the table, and slammed a math book on the table.

"Fine, then. I don't care what you do. I don't care if you ever get out of the fourth grade." She stared at me as I stomped up the companionway stairs to the deck.

Kate wrote to a friend in New York:

I am still in Isla. It is VERY boring. I'm the only kid here.

...My schooling is going this fast. SNAIL. I'll NEVER FINISH 4th Grade. Period. 4th Grade forever. Sounds like a book title...

She began signing her letters, "Fourth Grade Forever."

Over the next couple of months, my thoughts darted like ping-pong balls from one imagined scenario to another. I read about cruising the south coast of Cuba, and I looked up the international school in Havana where Kate's friend Laura had gone. We could live on the boat in a nearby port or maybe take an apartment while Kate was in school. I researched boarding schools in New England. I couldn't imagine sending Kate to one, but John's sister had gone, and he floated it as a possibility. I looked up schools in East Coast cities we had liked on the way down to Florida.

One day when Kate had a cold, she filled in the "Passage from" heading in the log with *Isla Mujeres,* the "to" heading with *Know-Where*, and the time as *8:50 Trying to not be a grump.* She wrote:

John is sick and grumpy. Susan is wearing a "I'll be cheerful if it kills me" expression, which at this rate, it will... I'll say this: we are not one happy family!

The foreign options wouldn't work. Kate wanted an American school. Although she knew a little Spanish, she stuck to English in Mexico and Guatemala and evinced no desire to mingle with local kids. We remembered the teenaged Canadian girl on the Rio Dulce who joined the Coast Guard because she couldn't fit into regular school anymore. We wanted to head back before it was too late.

John and I focused on three cities that we had all liked on the sail down—Annapolis, Charleston, and Fort Lauderdale—and rated them on a spreadsheet. Once we understood how cold Annapolis was in winter, we struck it from the list. We commenced research on the other two cities at the Internet cafe.

One day at the cafe, I stared at a list of Charleston

schools, my stomach churning. Soft bursts of Spanish rose above the clattering computer keys in the stale air. Across the room, Juliet researched shipping costs to Hong Kong for their boat. They had decided to ship the boat, so Mark could start his new job on schedule. We ran into each other daily at the cafe.

Juliet's cheerful, can-do attitude was the opposite of my melancholy mood. We took breaks from our research, exchanging what we had learned. Juliet's realistic outlook— no use crying, let's just get on and figure out the next bit— helped.

Finally, John and I made the fateful decision: we would sail back to Florida and explore Fort Lauderdale and Charleston in person. In May 1999, Cliff flew down, and we set sail from Isla Mujeres to Key West. The log notes from that trip are sparse, not much beyond latitude, longitude, and heading. On the way back, Kate wrote a poem about having to wear shoes again—shoes that pinch and squeeze, and laces that trip you. We had pressed onward for close to three years. It didn't feel right to head back and squeeze into ill-fitting shoes on land.

A dock sign in Key West greeted us: "No bare feet, no smoking, no dogs off leash—" My heart sank. We had sailed across seas without any guideposts. In Guatemala, we rode horses on the edge of a live volcano without any safety rails.

John wrote to Juliet and Mark:

...We have been here a bit over a week, intending to be here for a few days to get some through-hulls...and the air conditioning repaired...the air conditioning which hasn't worked since Belize, a year earlier, and which, Susan has told me a thousand times, MUST be repaired for us to exist in South Florida. And the refrigeration, of course. The refrigerator, which has not worked since the last 2 months in Isla Mujeres...sixty-three dinghy trips to the ice house, worked perfectly as soon as the US Refrigeration Expert from Sea Land Air Technologies climbed aboard...It must be some special aura US experts exude that scares the thing

into functioning...

Returning to the US has been difficult. The land of rules. I have already been threatened with being put in jail by a 5' 2" blond state trooper-ess named Officer Heidi. As you probably know, the traffic driving from Key West to Marathon is slow, especially at night. I attributed this slowness to the blue hairs and Floridians in general who don't know how to drive. Thus, to keep at a reasonable speed, I had to pass a number of cars and vans...repeatedly. I later found out that one set of vans that I passed was from the Florida Department of Corrections...

In the Land of Rules, we made our way to Fort Lauderdale. Kate wanted to go to an overnight summer camp, and we found a drama camp in the Adirondacks. Kate practiced the Happy Birthday song to audition for the musical. As usual, we hadn't thought too much about how the separation would affect us—we hadn't been apart in three years—or that Kate would not know anyone at the camp, and their backgrounds would be quite different from hers after living on a boat for three years. We hoped that a good dose of kids in a fun atmosphere would ease Kate's transition. We put her on a plane to New York, where Pat and Saron would take her to the camp bus.

Kate described camp in a letter home:

BUNKS: I am in Lower Stone House with:

Scoop (best friend, you'll meet her on Saturday)

Jaye (an idiot)

Whitenay (bug-eyed creep)

Mollie (butts into everyone's beeswax but okay)

Lola (HATE her)

Callie (she's okay)

Rachel (...a slob and snob and bickers)

Flora (Kill! Kill! Kill!)

Claire (cute and nice)

FOOD: I am starving. This morning, for instance, I get two tiny waffles, maybe the size of my hand, and a cut-up banana...Lunch is smaller. Snack. AGH!... Two cookies and a glass of Dimetapp. (That is what it tastes like)...

CIRCUS: It's okay. Terrifying. One kid, eleven, saw what trick he had to do and started to CRY. So now I'm stuck with the trick, and I know I will die.

This is camp. Can you pllleeeeeeeeeeaaase drive up before Saturday? ...I miss you so much, and I am totally forgotten around here...

Love, Kate

P.S. You WILL bring Elmo, right?

John and I scoured schools and houses in Fort Lauderdale and Charleston. We did not fare much better than Kate. We drove around with realtors in lovely neighborhoods but couldn't picture ourselves living in any of them.

We settled on Fort Lauderdale, a yachting center with a diverse population. We would live on the boat and hold off on the house search. After months of comparing schools, we chose a small private school that stressed individualized attention, again hoping to ease Kate's transition.

We attended Kate's circus performance at camp. Kate stood atop a wobbling pyramid of children—three bike riders on the bottom shakily whizzing around the ring, two children perched on their shoulders, and a deathly pale Kate on top. John and I froze, terrified for her. We met with the camp director, who pronounced Kate "really normal for a homeschooler." I understood then how casually educators would attach a stigma to homeschooling. It wouldn't matter if the child had sailed around the world, it was seen as a limitation of experience.

Before the school year started, John and I attended an orientation for parents at Kate's school. Kate was the only new fifth-grade student. We had thought that living on a boat in Florida—surrounded on three sides by water—would not be uncommon. Most of the parents, though, lived in interior suburbs with pools. My heart sank.

When I picked Kate up from the first day of school, her teacher said, "Kate's reading and writing are phenomenal. She'll need help with math, though."

Mrs. Kramer was in her thirties, tall and blond. Her dress was a little rumpled, her shoulders rounded, and her smile warm. Compared to the trim, well-dressed mothers, she looked refreshingly worn. As she talked, I remembered the piles of books we bought each visit home when we were cruising. I pictured Kate swinging back and forth for hours, bow to stern, ruminating about a novel.

Mrs. Kramer went on, "When I asked Kate to tell the class where she was from, she said, 'I'm from nowhere.'" We looked at each other and chuckled uncomfortably. Kate had told John and me that she had introduced herself that way at camp, too.

"Do you think Kate would like to talk to the class about where she's been?" Mrs. Kramer asked.

"I'm not sure. She really wants to fit in."

"It'll work out. She's already made friends with Molly." Mrs. Kramer smiled.

On the half-hour drive back to the boat, I asked, "So, how'd it go? Mrs. Kramer seems really nice." I glanced over at Kate. Her shoulders slumped into the seat. She looked tired.

"She is. Molly invited me over to play."

"That's good."

"These kids are such babies. They can't even cross the street by themselves." She took out a book and began to read.

"Maybe you just have to get to know them better."

"It won't matter. The girls were mean and wouldn't let me sit with them at lunch."

"It'll get better."

"No, it won't." She turned the page.

We drove for a while in silence down I-95 through the flat Florida landscape. The Northeastern etiquette of passing only from the left and slowing down to let in other cars didn't apply here. Cars sped up when you tried to shift lanes. As we passed the shopping malls and high-rises, I pictured Kate racing on the dinghy to visit Riley on *Big Easy*. They would head for shore, plotting their afternoon, Kate's dark hair and Riley's blond hair mingling in the wind. We were trying so hard here in Florida, but it felt all wrong.

Kate wound up hating that school. Other than Molly, most of the children were not allowed to play on the boat, even at the dock; the parents were afraid they would drown, which John and I found ridiculous. During that year, we enrolled Kate in a larger school where the children and parents were less insular.

We bought a house in a development in Delray Beach. I cried every night, missing the cruising life on *Laughing Goat* and our old lives in Connecticut. Desperate, I invited friends and relatives to visit but when they left, loneliness overcame me. We had no support system in Florida, no one to call in an emergency. I worried about what that might mean for Kate. I dreamed about the Fairfield house, no longer ours. Looking back years later, I wondered how I gave up so easily when John balked at moving back to Connecticut; at the time, I believed that it was a deal-breaker, and his identity depended upon leaving the old life behind. Maybe not, though.

A bright spot arrived in the form of Checkers, a jolly

Golden retriever puppy that we bought for Kate. He became Elmo's eager sidekick. I avoided the bible-thumping neighbors who reported on us whenever the dogs got loose. Every time I entered our code on the keypad and the entry gate shut behind us, I flinched at the irony of locking ourselves into our neighborhood.

Two years later in a local writing workshop, I began writing about the voyage—feverishly, waking up at all hours, trying to capture the feeling of meandering down the Intracoastal Waterway, sailing in following seas to Havana, fighting over math with Kate or crossing the sandbar to enter the Rio Dulce. Each moment of the voyage felt precious, a sweet voice from another world. John and I resolved that as soon as Kate graduated from high school, we would move back aboard a boat.

Chapter Twenty-Three
Elephants on the Horizon

Looking out to the horizon, it will appear jagged or saw toothed, large square waves (elephants), high seas kicked up by the determination of the stream, struggling to fight its way north against the wind. This is not the time to make your crossing.

— *http://www.cruisingguides.com/seadogblog/elepha nts-gulf-stream, simonscott 9/14/12)*

Eight years after we bought the house in Delray Beach, we sold it and moved aboard *Smooch*, a Norseman 40 catamaran, in Fort Lauderdale. Kate was a sophomore at college in New Orleans.

The sale unnerved her. She did not yet feel at home in New Orleans—that would happen a couple of years later. Unlike John and me, Kate was attached to the Delray Beach house, as I had been to the house in Fairfield. Guilt visited me for ripping her home away again. John pointed out that she was starting her own life now and would stay with us on the boat whenever she came home. We hoped in a couple of years to semi-retire in Central America.

A few months after moving aboard *Smooch*, we attempted to cross to the Bahamas. We had yet to sail in the dark without Cliff. Hearts thudding, we headed through Biscayne Channel, south of Miami, in darkness. We gave John's sister Pat instructions to call the Coast Guard if she didn't hear from us in twenty-four hours. As we edged further from shore, lumpy seas hampered our speed.

When the sky lightened, elephants—jagged waves that signaled turbulence in the Gulf Stream—marched across the horizon. We turned back about ten miles out. I declared victory. We had made it on our own out of the channel in the dark. New equipment, a GPS Chartplotter and radar, increased our confidence. Some weeks later, we left in the middle of the night and anchored outside Bimini by one o'clock in the afternoon.

"We did it!" I danced around the cockpit.

"It's about time," John said. "Now we can sail to Mexico by ourselves."

Over the next few years, we sailed to the Bahamas whenever we could, sometimes staying for a few months and exploring the islands while working remotely. In 2010, Elmo succumbed to cancer in the Bahamas. His loss devastated us, but at least he enjoyed the beaches he loved almost to the end. When John and I worked on a project in Europe, we docked the boat in Georgetown, Exumas, and Shae flew down to take care of Checkers, our golden retriever, while we were away. After Kate graduated from college, she found a job in New Orleans, a city that she had come to love.

One night, four years after we moved aboard, John shook me awake at midnight. We had just returned to Fort Lauderdale from a stint in the Bahamas. Still dressed, he turned on the light. "I think we should go to the hospital."

Blinking, I rose and leaned on an elbow. "It's gotten

worse?"

"Yeah."

He felt strange after dinner: heavy, maybe indigestion that he thought would go away.

I slid off the bunk and pulled on shorts and a top. John was already in the cockpit. Checkers wagged his tail on the bottom step, ready for a ride in the dinghy.

"Better tie the dog," John said as he loosened the dinghy. A soft breeze blew across the anchorage, and a lone car sped over the bridge from the beach road. I led Checkers up to the cockpit, tied him to the table, and helped John lower the dinghy into the water. He cranked the outboard.

"Do you think it's a heart attack?" I asked as we chugged through shards of pale, yellow moonlight scattered on the water.

"I don't know."

In the emergency room, a triage nurse hooked John up. Doctors and nurses sporadically checked on him. None would confirm whether or not he was having a heart attack. When dawn broke, John had had enough. He told a nurse that unless someone could illuminate what was going on, he was leaving. An ER doctor strode in.

"John, you can't leave. You're having a heart attack."

John and I looked at each other and laughed. John's firm stance while attired in a wrinkled hospital gown with dangling tubes had worked. A surgeon finally arrived. She would attach a catheter in John's leg, and most likely place a stent. I squeezed John's hand.

"See you in a little while." John returned a pained smile. He wanted this over with.

Hours went by. I checked John's status several times with little success. Eventually, I tracked someone down who accompanied me to the recovery room where John was sitting up in bed, ready to leave. They released him that afternoon.

John planned our departure for Mexico while the weather was favorable. I worried—my dad's heart attacks meant ambulances in the night, his face gray, my mother rushing to the hospital with him—but John said, "The problem is fixed." Still, it was already the first week of June, and the weather window for sailing to Mexico was closing. When John realized we would not complete repairs in time, he agreed to postpone the departure until hurricane season was over.

At John's follow-up cardiology appointment in November, his heart was fine, but a chest x-ray revealed a surprise: a mass in his lung. John wanted to go sailing and deal with the new problem later. The cardiologist insisted that John deal with it *now*.

John and I discussed ignoring the cardiologist's advice. We glared at the referral sheet. "Mass in left lung." We clung to hope, but there was only one disease it was likely to be. John wondered if it would make much difference if we took a couple of weeks to sail *Smooch* to Mexico. He had long maintained that he would die at fifty—he smoked three packs a day—and now, he was sixty-eight. Would a few weeks change anything?

We didn't sail. Maybe we could have had another adventure before the machinery of the oncological world kicked in. When John became a cancer patient, our world changed.

John chose an oncologist at MD Anderson in Orlando, three hours from Fort Lauderdale. At the first appointment, we parked the car and strolled toward the cancer center. Cadaverous patients in wheelchairs and bald women in headscarves crept along the sunny sidewalk. Our robustness shimmered inappropriately. We had recently sailed to the Florida Keys. We didn't belong here.

Dr. T. was petite and no-nonsense. She shook our hands and asked John how he felt.

"He's fine," I said. John glared at me.

Dr. T. requested a brain MRI and additional scans.

From what she had seen so far, the lung tumors were small but positioned close to a major artery. When John asked about his prognosis, she said that if John qualified for surgery, he had a thirty-five percent chance of success; if not, twenty-five percent.

Her words skittered through the air of the sterile room, precise words whose meanings eluded us. We nodded and asked questions, comprehending little. At sea, we relied on a flutter of the sail or ripples on the water to tell us where to steer, but in the cancer landscape, we were clueless.

On the way to the car, John asked me *never* to answer for him again. I apologized. He liked the blunt oncologist, whom he nicknamed Dr. Death. A week later, we met the wry radiologist on the team who believed that John's cancer was probably Stage 2—small and localized. Relieved, we ate lunch in the cafeteria before meeting again with Dr. Death.

That afternoon, Dr. Death pointed to a couple of tiny white specks amid black and white swirls and numbers on her computer screen. I had forgotten about the brain MRI that she requested. We stared at images of John's brain flecked with innocuous blobs. The lung cancer had traveled to the brain.

"The cancer is Stage 4," she said briskly.

John asked the reason for the classification. I cried, which normally would have horrified me. It was Stage 2 this morning; how did it become Stage 4 this afternoon? We learned that cancer traveling from its initial site is classified as Stage 4. I didn't hear much else that she said. Still reeling as we made our way to the brain radiologist, we hardly spoke.

Dr. R., the brain radiologist, deemed the tumors too small to treat. He was confident that if they grew, he could shrink or eliminate them with non-invasive surgery. I privately reclassified John's cancer to Stage 2, much as he remained blond to me long after his hair turned gray. The Stage 4 designation became immaterial, a technicality.

Despite my personal adjustment of John's cancer stage, time no longer stretched endlessly over the horizon. A wall sprang up ahead in the hazy distance like an impenetrable fog bank. When we had sailed in New England, we often ran into fogbanks, seeping gray mists that hardened into sheets with blue sky right up to the edge. When I recognized a telltale gray wall on the water, my stomach clenched, and fear would take over. I begged John to turn the boat around. But he sent me forward to keep a lookout, and on we would go. He took our bearings every few minutes, so we kept our course. Once we were in the fog and could see immediately around us, the fear abated. Moving forward cautiously was a template for facing danger.

A few weeks after the diagnosis, the day arrived for John's first chemo infusion, which would take several hours. Ensconced in a comfortable chair in a pleasant room with a few other chemo patients, he waited to be hooked up. The room felt—hopeful. As he worked on his computer, I stared at him. He suggested that I go for coffee or to shop. He saw no point in both of us being stuck there. At Starbucks down the street, I read the *New York Times*—relishing the rustling pages, which reminded me of Sundays in Fairfield with the paper spread out on the dining table alongside a plate of warm bagels.

When I returned an hour later, John was checking stocks on his computer. Other patients talked on the phone or chatted with relatives. I leaned forward and scrutinized John's face, waiting for mouth sores to erupt and burn in agony, or for what was left of his hair—a buzz cut—to fall out. He dozed. When he opened his eyes, I was still staring.

"How do you feel?" I asked, searching his face for changes.

"Okay. Cut it out."

Chemo, ports, scans, infusions. Drugs to combat nausea, constipation, diarrhea, swelling. The medications had to be given at precise intervals, one every six hours, another every four. I jotted down the times on a yellow pad. Dr. T. wanted John to drink sixty-four ounces of fluid each day to combat dehydration. I became John's note-taker, pharmaceutical manager, and post-chemo driver.

Our moods swung from day to day. In my journal, I noted:

So, after remaining relentlessly positive, even I wondered about it, people kept saying, call anytime, call if you need to talk, and I would think, talk? Why would I want to talk? ...fell into a funk last night...good to recognize...better to focus on John getting better...realized John seemed depressed...occurred to me, this must be getting him down...then I just felt bereft...like I'm about to lose him...well, that is what this kind of illness brings up, it brings death closer...need to allow myself to feel whatever it is, even the dark stuff...most of the time, I feel that this is something we're facing together as we've faced so many things... I count on John to charge ahead...which he's been doing...have to allow him not to feel positive all the time...because he certainly doesn't...yesterday was hard...but I...could drive the entire trip, from Orlando back to Fort Lauderdale, something I'd never done...usually John does most or all of the driving...

And, days later: *...there is this pressure in my head all the time... John's cancer...it's like a squeezing...constant...just want it to go away and everything would be like before...*

We brought Checkers with us on the trips to Orlando, and I walked him around the hospital grounds. His infectious joy not only lifted my spirits but also erased the troubled expressions of patients and staff alike. At home, Checkers helped, too. In early mornings as I wrote on my computer, Checkers slept under the table in the main salon, his chest rising and falling while I rubbed his belly with my foot and soaked up his warmth.

Usually so cheerful, Checkers was terrified of thunder.

One night when we were anchored in Coconut Grove, a storm came up while we slept, and he jumped off the boat. When we realized he was missing, John set out in the dinghy in the pouring rain to find him but had no luck. At daybreak, John searched the nearby shoreline. Frantic, we hung signs at marinas, stores, and parks. Later that day, we received a phone call from a golf club on Key Biscayne. Checkers swam ten miles across Biscayne Bay and splashed ashore on the first hole. Local TV and radio stations reported on our wonder dog's heroic swim.

But one day in March, a lethargic Checkers lay on the boat, feebly thumping his tail to say hi. On sunny days, we put him outside under a tree, hoping it would revive him. We drove him to the beach in the early morning past the red "No Dogs!" sign where he tried to romp.

Reluctantly, we took him to the veterinarian. Checkers had bone cancer. Although we both stayed with Elmo when the veterinarian in Nassau put him down three years ago, neither of us had the fortitude to stay this time. We went home and napped. When I woke up, I tripped on Checker's bald tennis ball and put away the red safety harness we had used to hoist him on the boat when his back legs stopped working. Without Checkers, the harness looked shabby and forlorn. We had to let him go, a loss, just when John and I needed him most.

After the fourth and last round of chemo, we received good news: John's tumor had shrunk. It had pulled away far enough from the artery to allow for surgery.

John had smoked since his teens. Cigarettes were as much a part of him as jeans and topsiders. By the time we met with the surgeon, John was so worried about the surgery that he smoked even more. The surgeon, who was going to remove half of John's left lung, said, "You have to quit smoking. This is a major operation. There is no point to it if you continue."

John had tried to quit before to no avail, but he asked for a prescription drug to help him, and quit. He never smoked again, nor stopped longing for a cigarette.

On the morning of surgery, six months after the diagnosis, I drove John to the hospital early. Talking with the surgeon ahead of time reduced our terror slightly. When the nurse wheeled John away, I steadied myself against a wall. John was in their hands now.

Pat, who lived outside of Orlando and with whom we stayed during John's treatments, joined me in the waiting room. To fill the time, we played a word game on my phone. Tinny musical notes gaily announced our correct answers, as other relatives anxiously murmured. Every so often, I rose to pour a stale cup of coffee and monitor John's progress on an electronic board above the nurse's station. I passed a table where a woman concentrated on a jigsaw puzzle with the same fierce frenzy as Pat and I played the word game.

After five hours, a nurse directed Pat and me to a hallway. "He's coming out now," she said.

The double doors swung open, and two technicians pushed a gurney through. The pale green walls peeled away, and I recognized John's feet—wide, high-arched, deck-calloused. He opened his eyes, as blue as the sea, and looked at me.

"I love you," he said groggily.

"I love you." We gazed at one another.

You're here. I'm back. I released my breath.

I held his eyes as Pat greeted him.

When they transported him to the recovery room, Pat said, "Did you see how my brother looked at you? He loves you so much. I'm grateful he has you."

Warmth flooded through me. Pat and I hugged. The crushing weight of the past months lifted for a second. Now, I'd like to reach back in time, smooth the forehead of my younger self, and squeeze Pat's shoulder. I would allow myself a few extra moments of release.

At John's two-month follow-up, the surgeon cleared

him for activity. Scans showed no new signs of cancer. Tasting the return of our old lives, I shut the cancer door with a satisfying click. If someone had asked me then whether John had a terminal illness, I would have said, "No." Maybe lung cancer in general was terminal. John's cancer was not.

Cancer returned on the next scans, two months later:

Awful day yesterday, this is all just so hard... Getting the plan for the radiation and chemo for the tumors in the lymph nodes...they're small... The radiologist says decent chance the radiation will cure them, meaning John's cancer won't appear in the lung/lymph node area anymore... Median is two years survival which at this point sounds good...so upsetting that these appeared so soon after surgery...these were missed...maybe too small yet to show up...then the awful news from Dr. R. that John's brain tumor grew and now has two others...still small but have to treat... We haven't told anyone yet...

Only thing to do is move ahead, one foot in front of the other...now have to figure out if we bring the boat up, where we stay, etc...

Two years, I'll go with that...

One foot in front of the other, we repeated to each other.

Dr. R. treated the brain tumors. Instead of sailing to the Bahamas, we would sail to Titusville on the Atlantic coast an hour east of Orlando for six weeks of lung radiation and chemo.

Ten months after the diagnosis, as we made our way up to Titusville, we were able to relax:

...nice to be on the water. Forgot how beautiful Florida is, the park around Hobe Sound, the little inlets, the birds, the people quietly fishing. It was such a good decision to do this rather than go to Pat's... We enjoyed anchoring every night. Felt normal for us.

On the second day of radiation, John, nauseous from chemo the day before, asked me to drive. Traffic choked the highway between Titusville and Orlando. As we crawled in the heavy traffic, John asked, "Do you plan to stay in this lane? You know you can switch, right?"

At the slightest opening in traffic, John, an aggressive driver, urged, "Go! Switch!"

I lurched recklessly from lane to lane. When we arrived at the hospital, I bumped over the curb and shooed him out, "Just get out, go, go!"

I parked the car and hunched over the steering wheel, weeping, for we had hounded each other, just like cancer hounded us.

John slept much of the time. The second and third weeks of radiation knocked him out completely. The radiologist likened the effect to a bad sunburn inside his chest and throat.

I would rise early and walk to a bridge that spanned the Intracoastal Waterway connecting the park near the marina to Cape Canaveral. I looked out to sea at passing boats and checked the shuttle launchpads, visible from the top of the bridge. On a bench, I meditated.

During my walks, I slipped the bonds of time and space. John's illness disappeared. On the way home, I bounded down the ramp to the dock, and my steps slowed. Back on the boat, John's distress jarred my buoyant mood. His misery didn't fit in my illusory morning world.

One day—a day off from radiation—John asked if he could join me on the walk. He usually didn't have the stamina for more than a quick stroll around the marina. Thrilled that he felt better, I drove to the bridge. As we slowly climbed the bridge, John said, "We need to talk."

He continued, "I don't think I'll live as long as you're imagining. We need to figure out a Plan B."

Why was he bringing this up *now*? Didn't we have enough to deal with just to get through the radiation? I reiterated that the *median* was two years of survival. He had just as good a shot of being on the long side. His pointed stare silenced me.

"I haven't slept for a week worrying about us." In the quiet, seagulls cawed, and a car passed. Smells of the sea and sweet grasses in the park floated over. The sun shone in a bright blue sky.

I said, "You mean, a plan for *me*?"

For after he was gone? I couldn't think about that now.

"Well, that, too, but I meant, another plan for us." He smiled at my shell-shocked expression. "We don't have to talk about it now. Just think about it."

"Okay," I said.

At the time, I blamed him for insinuating dark thoughts into the sunny morning. I wanted to convince him that he was wrong, that we had at least two years. Now, I look back and feel his alarm. I imagine his internal monologue, worrying about me and thinking about how to get through to me. He knew what I was so assiduously avoiding: he was going to leave me. He didn't want to, but it was going to happen.

As the weeks of radiation continued, John's pain worsened. From the spot on the settee where he napped during the day, he said, "If I'm going through all this and all I get is three months, it's not worth it."

The radiation ended, but as John recovered, he caught pneumonia, delaying the follow-up chemo. We were stuck in Titusville for another couple of months.

The four-day sail home to Fort Lauderdale was not as pleasant as the trip up. Sailing exhausted John. We anchored each night, had dinner, and went to sleep. As was his habit, John entered a brief note in the log before bed. He didn't have the energy to rant as he had in the *Laughing Goat* log, but he kept a diligent record. He would not have forgiven himself for falling short on his duty to the boat.

We arrived at our dock in Fort Lauderdale. A visiting friend caught our lines. He and his girlfriend had sold their boat and moved to Europe. We had not seen him for a year. He was one of the few people with whom John could while away hours talking politics, boats, and life. Although trying to remain cool, he looked shocked at John's appearance, which in turn, shocked me. I was glad that John was too tired to notice.

One year and a month had passed since the diagnosis.

During the next six months, we sped back and forth to Orlando for scans, chemo, and MRIs. John tackled the Orlando runs like speed races, burning up I-95 at ninety miles per hour. Inside the car, I gripped the sides of the passenger seat. The seat belt felt as insubstantial as a shoelace. Every lane change, I gasped and shrieked.

"Your reaction makes it worse. I can't concentrate," John said, accusing me of over-dramatizing.

"Slow down, please just slow down," I begged, clutching the seat, hardly breathing.

"Don't worry. It's under control. You know I'm a really good driver." He *was* a good driver. John enjoyed driving.

But that wasn't the point. He wasn't responding to my entreaties. He dismissed my feelings. I kept my eyes peeled on the speedometer. When it strayed above ninety, I pointed at it. He slowed down—to ninety.

Even two $300 speeding tickets did not deter John. After several hair-raising rides, I gave up trying to slow John down. Instead, I took a sedative before we set out. I had turned to tranquilizers in my thirties to bolster my confidence when I gave a speech at a packed advertising conference. At his pressure-filled ad agency, John had used them occasionally, too. We kept a stash on hand, renewed at our annual physicals.

Looking back, I'm struck by John's single-mindedness. He probably would have preferred driving alone. He didn't have room right now for my feelings.

When his PET scan report stated "no evidence of disease" for the first time in months, we looked ahead to the future. We hadn't worked since treatment began a year and a half ago. We had depleted our savings. John suggested living somewhere cheaper. He wanted to enjoy life, rather than waiting around Florida for the results of each scan.

Smooch, which we had planned to sail through Central America, now remained at the dock. A thick layer of algae bloomed at the waterline.

One day over lunch at a favorite spot, a campy gay bar and restaurant, John suggested selling the boat. The air went out of the room. I had thought of it, too, but hadn't said anything. I could hardly look at him. I said, "Are you sure?"

With a weary glance, he nodded. If his condition worsened, he did not want me to be stuck handling the boat myself. He would not have mentioned it unless he had given it careful thought. Seated amid over-the-top paintings, bespangled waiters, salacious sayings, and tropical foliage, I felt bereft, as though we were leaving a child we loved behind.

Over the next few weeks, we read about expatriate communities in Mexico, Nicaragua, and Ecuador, and contacted hospitals about cancer treatment costs and insurance in those countries. We talked to bankers and yacht brokers. Reluctantly, we put the boat on the market.

By the end of August, *Smooch* was under contract. After we accepted the offer, *Smooch* wasn't big enough for both of us.

We drove to Key West for a few days to get away from the boat. On the drive down, John said, "I'm on the verge of a nervous breakdown." He longed for a cigarette, reaching into his pockets, and coming up empty-handed.

For several days, we bickered. John wanted to break the contract and sail to the Bahamas. He brought up assisted suicide and asked me to promise that if his health got worse, we would move to one of the states where it was legal. I hadn't realized he was focusing on what I believed was still on a distant horizon.

One day over lunch, we watched boats sail out of the sunny harbor as waiters rushed by with heaping platters of fried clams and scallops. Amid tourists' carefree laughter, we spoke quietly, our energy spent.

"I hate the idea of being without a boat," John said.

"I do, too."

"I'm no longer an ad guy. Without a boat, I'll have no identity."

I thought of John's lifelong sailing dream. Without it, what would keep him going?

By the end of the trip, we agreed that it made sense to honor the contract and sell the boat. In September, one year and nine months after diagnosis, we sold *Smooch* to a world-famous single-handed sailor who was launching a charter company in Puerto Rico. We moved into a rental cottage.

The next MRI results showed that the surgery had demolished the latest brain tumors:

And the best news yesterday...they got that fucker brain tumor... Dr. R. said the results could not have been better...it is a little corpse now...and nothing new popped up...and he showed us how all the others that have been treated are still tiny... He said, I have nothing to treat... John goes back in three months...

With a three-month reprieve, our spirits lifted. We found a clinical trial in Miami for immunotherapy, a promising new treatment, and tendrils of hope sprang up anew. When John was accepted, we felt like we had won the lottery.

We found a spectacular house in Merida, Mexico. For half the cost of renting a studio apartment in South Florida, we would have an elegant three-bedroom home in the heart of the city with a beautiful garden and pool. We would rent it for one month to give ourselves a chance to try out life in Merida, and if we liked it, rent a place with a longer lease.

We spent a couple more months winding down our affairs and preparing to move. John had another clean brain scan. For the moment, our two sources of worry and fear— cancer and financial ruin—were in abeyance. In April 2015, two years and four months after the diagnosis, we moved to Mexico, hope on the rise again.

Chapter Twenty-Four
Merida

In our house on Calle 55, a quiet street in the historical center of Merida, I danced from room to room in my sarong. We took Spanish lessons two mornings a week in a bakery where we ordered cappuccino brewed with Chiapas coffee, while John and another student, a wisecracking retired lawyer from Philadelphia, mercilessly teased the good-natured young teacher. We shopped at the market in Parque de Santiago, where after picking out mangos and avocados, we ordered carnitas tacos with tender, braised-for-hours pork at the taco stand. On Sunday mornings, we strolled on Paseo Montejo, a broad leafy avenue in the style of the Champs Elysees in Paris. In passing, friendly Maya smiled and asked, *"Como esta?"*

John had not cooked for months in Florida but made dinner in Merida a couple of times a week. Puttering in his sarong, he brined pork butt and cooked it slowly, bubbling in its fat on top of the stove. His favorite spot in Merida was a farmer's market downtown, a warren of bustling stalls selling everything from pig's heads to furniture sprawled over several city blocks. John joked with fishmongers and photographed shoppers among rows of glistening grouper fillets and octopuses' dangling arms.

With temperatures in May climbing to 115 degrees, middle-aged ex-pats skinny-dipped at home in small, cool plunge pools. In the pool, John's legs did not hurt but walking to the nearby market on the narrow, uneven sidewalks, his legs ached. At home, he napped on the couch while I lounged on the patio among lush plants, flowers, and the jewel-like pool. I marveled at our good fortune.

John's first trip home for treatment went smoothly. At the end of the first month, we knew we had made the right decision to come to Merida. The fabulous house we were renting was unavailable for a longer term. We found another house with a six-month lease. Though small and cluttered compared to the house on Calle 55, it had a pool and pots of fragrant night-blooming cacti outside the front door.

However, John's CT scan showed possible lung tumor growth. The doctor told us that, best case, it was inflammation, a sign that the immunotherapy was working. It was too soon to tell. A wise friend with lymphoma had once said that whenever the doctors presented a benign explanation, she would take it. For now, we accepted inflammation as the culprit.

In late afternoons while John slept, I shopped for dinner. One day, walking home from the market in the oppressive heat, the shopping bag weighing me down, and a heat rash chafing my thighs, I leaned against a building. A friend in an air-conditioned car stopped for me, and I wept with gratitude. Another day, in yoga class, I lay quietly with my thoughts while pressure bore down on my back like a giant hand.

I found an Al-Anon group that met in the Merida English Library, a lovely colonial building. John went to an AA group there at the same time. The Al-Anon group met in an exquisite room with floor-to-ceiling books and a round glass table with bright cloths. When we closed the carved wooden door to begin, a hush would descend. Worries about John's health that I held at bay all week floated free, and I felt safe to talk about them.

The news about John's lungs remained murky. Determined to take each day as it came, we visited friends at the beach, traveled to an undeveloped island in the Gulf of Mexico, and a UNESCO World Heritage city on the Yucatan Peninsula.

In August, now two years and eight months since the diagnosis, we heard from the conferring oncologists. The immunotherapy was not working. The lung tumors had grown. John would have to go back on chemo, which he dreaded. As John told me the news, a bird sang. The carefree sound angered me. Cancer tightened its grip again.

My birthday was coming up, so I made reservations for our traditional fall trip visiting Raegan in Maine, Kate in New Orleans, and a friend in New York. We could sandwich the visits in between two of John's treatments.

About midway through the flight to Miami, John's coughing reached a crescendo. He could not catch his breath. His face turned white. Wondering if there was a doctor on the flight, I reached for the call button. John swatted my hand down and told me not to worry. After we arrived in Miami, John lurched down the aisle, and we sat in the first seats we found at the gate.

"Do you want a wheelchair?" I asked.

"No!"

Adamant, he shuffled through endless corridors, leaning on my arm, and sitting down frequently. His frailty surprised me, compared to a similar visit a year ago.

John had a pre-chemo appointment with Dr. R., the Miami oncologist, who took one look at John's ashen face and asked, "Do you want me to admit you to the hospital?"

I started to shout "Yes!" but John shot me a warning glance. He had no intention of staying in the hospital. Dr. R. treated his congestion and made an appointment with a pulmonologist for the next morning.

We arrived in New Orleans to stay at a charming Airbnb cottage tucked among oak trees and pink azaleas. Kate dropped by to check on us. John's medical contraptions and pills dominated every surface. Happy to see her dad, Kate sat with him on the bed where he was resting and joked about the surfeit of medications.

Kate took off from work during the week, and we rode a steamboat on the Mississippi. We poked fun at the other tourists and enjoyed being on the water together. Kate's boyfriend's parents invited us to dinner. His Spanish mom would cook her special flan. When John heard about the flan, he was determined to make his equally renowned key lime pie.

John and I shopped for ingredients, borrowed cooking equipment from Kate, and set to work in the minuscule cottage kitchen. Pans, bowls, limes, boxes of ginger snaps and gelatin, and bags of pecans and sugar covered every inch of space. Between napping and inhaling medications, John beat, whipped, and mashed ingredients. John's tenacity again astonished me. We did not have the right beater for the whipped cream—but he pressed on. John's pie was a hit.

The next day, we flew to New York. Over a couple of days, we squeezed in lunches, dinners, and museums with friends and relatives. The trip so far had been a relay race. In our room, John would sit with a whirring nebulizer and medicinal vapors before we dashed off for our next date. We fell into bed exhausted at night.

In Maine, we had a breather and relaxed for a few days. Then, we flew to Orlando for John's chemo. A brain MRI, though, indicated a tumor that required immediate surgery again. A six-month lease on our current house in Merida ended that week, and we planned to move into a different house for the next six months. John stayed with Pat and Fred while I flew back to pack and move. I would return to Orlando for the surgery.

Home in Merida, I had three days to move. Though he couldn't help it, John had stuck me with the packing again. At the next Al-Anon meeting, I couldn't wait to tell my friends how well I was managing. I described the awful plane ride, the rushing, the unexpected brain tumor, and now, the packing. They stared at me, kindness and disbelief written on their faces. I slumped to the table, crying.

I said, "I'm stressed out." They nodded.

Relief flooded through me. I had been so tightly holding myself together. Now, I could not ignore the toll the trip had taken, and how much harder it was than the same trip just one year ago. When I told John about it later on the phone, he said, "You can live under stress and handle it while simultaneously feeling the stress. That's how most people live."

For years, John had maintained that life had gray areas, that all was not black and white. But I didn't quite believe that. Denial helped me cope.

We moved into the new house, a spacious aerie like the first house on Calle 55, with freshly painted white walls, comfortable couches and chairs, and bright pillows arrayed in the living room and den. The house and garden radiated serenity, with a few tasteful paintings amid cool white expanses. Upstairs, the master bedroom had a large, tiered terrace with lounges, trees, and flowers. Birds twittered in fruit-laden trees.

The first week of December, while John was in Miami for the next chemo and scan, I went to a yoga class. After class, a new friend and I had coffee at a bistro. In the courtyard among palms, tiled tables, and wall paintings of Frida Kahlo, I poured forth my worries about John's cancer. I hardly paused for breath. When I wound down a half-hour later, we both laughed. I had not realized how much I needed to talk. Another friend joined us after class the following week, and we became a trio, meeting regularly over coffee.

Both were retired nurses, realistic and comfortable talking about illness. I came to depend on our coffee sessions.

One day at the bistro, one of the women asked, "Do you need to talk to someone?"

She meant someone professional. A spark of resentment flared up at the suggestion. I was doing fine that day. John and I had just had good news—the tumors had shrunk with the new chemo. But, thinking of the ups and downs of the past months, I reconsidered.

A liberal Roman Catholic priest from Portugal who had a doctorate in psychology and spoke several languages lived in an older section of town. When he opened the heavy wooden door to his home, his warm smile put me immediately at ease. He became my shrink-priest.

We sat in an open high-ceilinged library with floor-to-ceiling bookshelves, a beautiful wood desk, and an inviting lived-in couch. Small tables, stacks of books, paintings, and pottery filled in the room. He offered me a coffee on a silver tray. Grace, civility, and calm bathed the room.

I told him about John's cancer and our years of sailing. He asked about our children and my family. I sniffled into a Kleenex from a box on the table.

He said, "You've had a rich life, lived consciously. Here in Merida, you think your life sailing with John is all behind you. But it is alive inside of you."

I could not stop crying. We had lived through uncertainty and had weathered other storms. A new life in Merida would not change all that had come before. I told him about a feeling lately of being chased, peering over my shoulder looking for someone, and the relentless hand pressing down on my back.

He said, "Time is chasing you."

I could not escape. But I was not in denial anymore, at least for the moment.

I walked a dozen blocks home, my steps lighter, my love for John shining bright. The shrink-priest had asked about my relationship with my dad and suggested talking to my father about John. I looked up past the colorful houses, windows flung open to the breezes, and the tattered, cheerful tienda signs, and I began a conversation with my father.

"Hi, Dad! I think you would like it here." My dad had loved Miami Beach, a respite from Ohio's winter chill. I pictured my dad enjoying the street scene as I did—families seated near their front doors fanning themselves, gossiping and eating while children played. I imagined my father and me as adults, and my dad's presence soothed me.

He answered, "Susie, look around you. What a place! So colorful. If John could get better anywhere, it would be here."

Merida celebrated the Noche Buena festival that weekend. Art galleries all over the city opened their doors with new exhibits, and music and wine flowed. Friends invited us to gallery-hop that evening. John didn't feel well enough but told me to go ahead.

I wanted to, but after indulging in a few moments of self-pity for my lost night on the town, I realized that I would rather be home with John. I made dinner, and we retired to the couch in the den. I nestled into John's shoulder, his arm around me, and we watched two episodes of "Good Wife." Nestling into John was my most comfortable place to be.

John felt better in the morning, and we decided to go to an art exhibit. After viewing the work of a young Cuban artist, we headed down a side street in search of a taxi. John was making tentative progress when a coughing spasm overtook him. Doubled over, he couldn't catch his breath. He collapsed against a brick building. No one else was around. As he went down, I wondered what to do: call the emergency police number or our wisecracking friend who had offered to be our *ambulancia*?

John rose, still shaky, and continued walking. Rooted to the spot, now *I* could not move. I wanted to go home, but John wanted to go out to lunch. We caught a taxi to an ex-pat hangout near our house, where we split a burger and watched a football game on TV.

During the night, John's coughing woke me up. He went back to sleep, but I sat on the sofa downstairs, peering through the sliding doors into the moonlit garden. I couldn't stop thinking about the moment John keeled over against the building. Daily excursions had become fraught with danger. I was out of my depth. John didn't even have a doctor here. I didn't want to lose him on a side street in Merida.

Christmas approached. Kate and her boyfriend Alex were coming. Raegan and her children would visit, too. Kate arrived a few days early. She approved of our spacious house and new lifestyle.

John drove Kate and me to a cenote, a deep freshwater pool found in limestone caverns throughout the Yucatan located on the edge of town. When we arrived, he told us to walk ahead. As Kate and I made our way along the flowered path, she said, "Poor Dad."

John was her ski and scuba diving buddy, the boat captain leading us into the unknown. Now, he walked too slowly to keep up with us. As Kate and I swam among the lily pads, though, John waved from the path.

Alex arrived, and John drove us to Uxmal, the ruins outside of Merida. After parking the car, we climbed a winding uphill path to the entrance. At the Nunnery Quadrangle, John announced that he was tired and would go no further. He headed back to the entrance to wait for us at a cafe.

Later, though, we spied him ahead, red-faced, and out of breath. I ran toward him. He asked, "Where the hell is the exit?"

John, who had found his way across the Gulf of Mexico, had wandered in circles. I joined him on the trail back to the entrance, and we rested in a quiet clearing on a bench at a ranger's station. A nearby stream trickled, and bushes whispered in a light breeze. John reached for my hand.

"Thank you for being here for me." He squeezed my hand and sighed.

"Of course."

I ran my fingers along his arm, over bumps and bruises from chemo and blood thinners. The sailor's tan had faded. Everything was much closer to the surface now. We sat still, taking in the quiet.

He said, "I knew you would be." I looked at him. "Because of sailing." He smiled.

I held onto his hand and rested my head on his shoulder. In my twenties, when I was so needy, I would never have imagined that I would be there for him.

Raegan and her children arrived. John led them through the labyrinthine downtown *mercado,* and we went out to favorite restaurants. A high point of the week: John's arm-wrestling match with Raegan over dinner, a longstanding tradition, in which John prevailed and cackled victoriously.

L'Chayim, my dad might have said.

On we go.

John slept for a couple of days after they left. His cough worsened, and he shivered uncontrollably. The shaking scared me. We headed to Orlando for John's chemo, and Dr. T. treated him for pneumonia. Once again, her quick reaction relieved my anxiety.

John consulted a throat surgeon, who agreed to operate on his paralyzed vocal cord, which was causing voice problems. The operation would be in two weeks. Rather than wait, we flew back to Merida. Pat offered to take John to the operation when he returned, and I would not have to buy another plane ticket.

After John left again for Florida, I moped and worried about how he would get along without me. My new Spanish teacher, an anthropologist, had a last-minute cancellation for a trip she was leading to Chiapas, a remote Mexican state that bordered Guatemala. It sounded interesting—religious festivals, intricate textiles, Mayan ruins. John would not have the stamina now for such a trip. With encouragement from my shrink-priest, I signed up.

I stayed in the jungle with the Lacandon tribe, the only Maya unconquered by the Spanish. I took part in religious festivals in mountain villages alive with townspeople in gorgeous hand-woven costumes, with masses of flowers on display, firecrackers popping, incense perfuming the air, and music blaring in the square. At the same time, town elders paraded with religious icons. I strolled San Cristobal de las Casas, the sophisticated Chiapas capital in the mountains. I rode a boat down the Usumacinta River that bordered Mexico and Guatemala to Yaxchilan, Mayan ruins entered through a labyrinth where howler monkeys shrieked, and Maya families worshiped at sacred ceiba trees.

At other Mayan ruins, I had rarely attempted climbing the steps, but at Yaxchilan, I trotted up hundreds of steps to the temple. I maintained a steady pace upward, liberated from my usual fear of heights. I sniffed the cool, fresh air at the top and flashed a victory sign to the small figures in the grass below. I strutted around admiring the view.

I spoke to John before the throat surgery. He sounded hopeful. I wished I could be with him. That night, I had a nightmare. I was with a group of people I didn't know well, and Geena Davis, the movie star, handed me a baby to hold. I kept losing it and heard later that the baby was murdered. I woke up screaming. I was supposed to be home taking care of John.

When I got home from Chiapas, John was home and had his voice back, but he had caught a virus and felt terrible. I stayed in my pajamas all weekend and dreamily sorted through photographs from the trip while John slept. A jaguar sculpture I bought in Chiapas gazed fiercely into the garden from the coffee table in the living room.

John hardly left the house all week and weakened by the day. Desperate, I booked flights to Orlando again for John and me. As soon as we arrived at Dr. T.'s office in

Orlando, she admitted John to the hospital. John was near kidney failure.

Cancer was gaining ground.

After Dr. T.'s treatment, John got better, but my anxiety ratcheted up when we returned home to Merida, far from the medical expertise in Orlando. We would be on our own again.

One day, when John declined to go out, I asked why he was scowling. He said, "I'm so sick of feeling sick."

My heart dropped. John had endured so much without complaint. I latched onto moments when John was not suffering as proof that he was getting better, but every day brought fresh trials—a nosebleed, nausea, breathing difficulties. We signed with an insurance agent who offered health services to ex-pats for emergencies.

Now three years and three months after the diagnosis, John awakened the day before he had to leave for chemo in Orlando in March too dizzy to lift his head. I booked a flight to Orlando to accompany John the next day. John had an MRI, and we met with Dr. R., the brain radiologist. On Dr. R.'s computer, white blobs of all sizes glowed like misshapen stars from the dark recesses of John's brain— new tumors. John would need two weeks of whole-brain radiation to zap them. Dr. R. asked John not to fly for two months.

Dr. R. said, "The next two months will be a delicate time for the brain, a little dicey."

John's interpretation: "Your brain will explode if you fly."

Dr. R. was confident that he could keep John's brain clear of tumors for six months or longer, and if new ones cropped up, he would again perform Gamma Knife surgery. He wanted to begin immediately.

I recoiled from the term "whole brain radiation." I imagined John becoming a vegetable. Dr. R. assured us that would not happen. He would prescribe medication that would prevent cognitive loss.

We held onto the hope that Dr. R. would perform his magic: John would come through this terrible turn of events intact, a little the worse for wear.

"Cheated death again!" I proclaimed, but it was as though I said it into the wind. John smiled weakly.

Kate visited. Throughout John's illness, Kate had insisted on being part of the medical side of things. Whenever John had a doctor's appointment, we awaited our ringing phones, knowing that Kate would call to find out what was going on.

The nurse, Kate, and I entered the radiation chamber with John. Signs on the bare walls blared radiation dangers in large red letters. A gleaming metal structure dominated the middle of the room. The nurse encased John's head in a mask so he could not move, strapped him down, and wheeled him to the machine. Then, the nurse, Kate, and I fled.

"Bye, Dad. Love you."

"Love you, John."

In the waiting room, Kate cried, thinking of her dad alone, trapped, and bombarded with toxic rays in a harsh, cold environment. I had become inured to the brutal cancer protocols, as though they had no effect on my feelings, but for her, it was a fresh assault.

John took the brain radiation well: a little unsteady on his feet, yet his brain remained sharp. We would return to Merida as soon as the doctor cleared him to fly.

Chapter Twenty-Five
Gone

Dr. T. recommended that John find a primary physician. I had not seen a doctor myself for several years, and we both made appointments for physicals.

My new doctor, a young woman with a dazzling smile, swept into the examining room and asked, "How are you?" Sobbing, I told her about John's illness. In three years of accompanying John to doctors, I had never discussed my health. My doctor prescribed some tests and suggested that I would benefit from talking to a clinical social worker.

I said, "We're going back to Merida soon, so it's not really worth it."

She said, "Well, you're here *now*."

I called the social worker.

At our first meeting, the social worker explained anticipatory grief, which begins while your loved one is still present. Each day, thoughts and dreams assailed me that I pushed aside. From the kitchen, I stared at John's back as he worked on the porch in ninety-degree heat in his red sweatshirt, fleece-lined and hooded from L.L. Bean, hanging loosely now on his thinning shoulders. He could never warm up enough. I imagined him fading away—too terrifying a thought to wrap my mind around. I bawled.

At night, John no longer slept on his back, facing outward, arm around me, pulling me into his chest. Now, he curled up in a fetal position, his back to me, pale shoulders rounded inward. Up until the last couple of months, we had enjoyed an active sex life. One night, I asked him about it.

"Do you think you'll want to have sex again?" John sighed and lifted the top sheet to look down his body.

"Yes! I keep checking, but nothing is going on down there."

We laughed ruefully. I missed my broad-shouldered tanned sailor. We were threading our way onward through ever-narrowing reef passages.

I worked on jigsaw puzzles constantly. I would leave one out on the dining table, a work in progress. Pat and Fred would add to it during the day. I loved jigsaw puzzles, inching steadily toward greater clarity. Progress had a different meaning with cancer, where tumors progressed as cancer advanced. When we completed a puzzle, we cheered for ourselves and started a new one.

The social worker encouraged me to share my feelings with John soon.

"Why?" I asked.

"Things can change quickly. If there's something you want him to know, tell him before it's too late."

Too late? Despite the latest setbacks, I still imagined years ahead together.

One day on the way to lunch, when we stopped at a light, I said, "I have something to tell you."

John peered ahead over the steering wheel, listening.

"I love you, and I'm going to miss you so much." Through tears, I continued, "And I just wanted to say…"

John interrupted, "I'm hesitating because I understand

how important it is for you to get out your feelings. But... I'm *still* here!"

I nearly choked with laughter at my earnest attempt to reveal to John what he already knew, what we lived in our bones: I loved John in a realm beyond words.

On the morning of the appointment in Orlando for the MRI results, John handed me the car keys, a formal acknowledgment that I had taken over the driving. The keys felt clunky in my hand, and I almost dropped them. John said, "I don't trust my legs anymore."

We pulled up to the valet stand at the hospital. I raced to the restroom. When I came out, I could not find John. He was not in the lobby or the radiology wing. He did not answer his phone. Through the lobby window, I spotted our car, which should have been in the garage by now. John's knees poked out from khaki shorts on the ground; blue-garbed medical personnel milled around. I rushed outside.

Seated on the pavement, John leaned back, oddly at ease against the rear car door. We glanced at each other for a second, his blue eyes as piercing as ever. An oxygen tank lurked nearby, and a tube snaked into his nose.

Out of breath, I identified myself to the group. A tech explained that John had blacked out during a coughing fit as he climbed out of the car and fell to the pavement. John insisted he was fine and wished to leave for his appointment. I berated myself for rushing off, oblivious to John's distress.

The tech pointed to the oxygen tank.

"We need to admit you to the emergency room where we can monitor you." Gentle murmurs from the others echoed her words.

John suggested that they let him sit for a moment to catch his breath, so he could keep his doctor's appointment. I admired his resolute stance. He wasn't going quietly. He continued to negotiate while around us, cars discharged patients, doctors rushed between buildings, and valets sprinted to the garage.

Eventually, John agreed to be admitted to the ER. John was still in the emergency room waiting for a bed to open up on the floor when I left later that night to go back to Pat's. I didn't want to leave him there. If only John could have steered us clear of this obstacle as he would on the water.

The next day, Dr. T., John's oncologist, strode into the room. The tests she had ordered showed new lung tumors pressing on John's airway. A surgeon would dig out as much as he could and stretch a balloon in John's airway to help him breathe.

Underneath the matter-of-fact discussion coursed the new knowledge that cancer had spread through the lung and that the current chemo treatment was not working. Dr. T. would present us with treatment options after the surgery. Unfortunately, the only surgeon who performed the airway operation was on vacation. John would have to stay in the hospital until the surgeon returned in a week. Given his breathing difficulties, it was too risky to release him.

To add to the misery, John caught C diff, a highly contagious hospital infection. To enter his room, we had to suit up in gowns, gloves, and slippers. The nurses changed the sheets half a dozen times a day. I washed the dirty underwear at home and rinsed Pat's washing machine with bleach.

The surgery was successful. At John's follow-up appointment with Dr. T., she explained that between the new lung tumors and the brain tumors, which could crop up again, only one chemo treatment remained, with a five percent chance of success.

"It's not a great choice, and I can't begin the treatment until the C diff is completely gone."

We stared at her, struck dumb. John asked Dr. T. about clinical trials.

"You've had so many lines of treatment by now, you'd be flying all over the country to find one that you'd qualify for. You could do it, but it would be hard on you."

As the clock above the door ticked, the room's silence enfolded us.

Dr. T. said, "If you don't want to go ahead, it would be understandable. In that case, you should consider hospice. You don't have to decide this second."

John and I followed the nurse out of the examining room. The intense quiet and the blue-tinged light in the clean fluorescent-lit hallway usually gave me hope, but today, alarm bells clanged through my body. John stumbled, and I reached for him, but he shook me off and leaned against the beige wall.

The nurse and I strode ahead chatting about the weather. I had one ear attuned to John's steps behind us. I feared he would fall again.

After the nurse retreated, I pressed the elevator button. To the screams of "The View" audience from TVs in the background, we searched each other, settled on each other. John rested his hand on my shoulder, and we entered the elevator going down.

On the drive to Pat's house, John slept. The next morning, he recalled Dr. A., a leading cancer researcher in Tampa, who had asked John to call him when the chemo stopped working. John wanted to try that next.

"But what about Dr. T.?" I asked.

"It's my body."

I drove John to Tampa for the appointment with Dr. A. As we waited for the doctor, John fell asleep. Dr. A. had an opening in a new trial, but John had to completely eradicate the C diff before he could start.

At home, John slept. I wanted to wake him, take him out to lunch, and talk about politics or the Pulse nightclub shooting, which had occurred last week in Orlando. I missed John's perspective. Instead, I did errands and jigsaw puzzles and went out to lunch with Pat and Fred.

For the first time, John had no appetite and lost weight.

The people running the trial in Tampa called and left messages, which I didn't answer. Almost as an afterthought, John and I decided that we would not go back to Mexico to live. We would find a temporary place in Tampa while John was in the trial.

When I roused him for an appointment with Dr. T. in Orlando, he could not stand up or walk straight. He sank into a chair in Pat's living room. His face looked gray.

"Are you okay?" I asked.

He nodded. I wanted him to tell me what to do. I thought of bundling him into the car and speeding to Orlando, but I wasn't sure he could make the trip.

I called 911, another first. My brother-in-law Fred ran out to the driveway to wave in the ambulance, his arms circling as though landing a plane. I stood at the door, one eye on John, one on Fred waving.

In the truck, they defibrillated John and rushed him to the ER at the hospital in The Villages, where Pat and Fred lived. Fred and I jumped in the car to meet them there. Pat joined us in the hospital waiting room. I had little faith in the hospital or its doctors. I wanted John under Dr. T.'s care in Orlando, but she said that it was not advisable to move him. She would consult with the doctors in The Villages.

At the hospital, the doctors surmised that a clot blocked John's artery. In a room in the ER, John looked dazed, but he was sitting up. As usual, John was ready to leave, though in no condition to go anywhere.

The next day, John still was not eating. When I asked if he could eat something, he drowsily shook his head.

The cardiology team swept into the room. A cardiologist cheerily announced that they had fixed the clot. He drew a diagram on a whiteboard to show me that John was out of danger. But John was barely conscious, and not eating or drinking. The cardiologist's breezy confidence stirred up my stored anger at hospitals, doctors, cancer, and C diff. What a joke that the doctor thought that he had fixed John. The clot now seemed immaterial. John was fading away by the minute.

I took a break outside and called Dr. T.

"He looks awful," I said, my voice quivering. "He hasn't eaten for days. I don't know what to do about the trial."

My eyes were closed as I listened to her, calm and competent, in the gathering dusk. She had unstintingly done the right thing for John for three and a half years.

She said, "I worry that John is not strong enough now to take part in the trial."

As soon as she said it, I knew she was right.

She said, "He's where he needs to be."

She would continue to consult with the doctors and again mentioned hospice.

It seemed like the end—but it had felt like the end before. What if John just needed sustenance, and he would revive? Later that night, I called the hospital and, after several tries, spoke with the doctor in charge of John's care.

"My husband hasn't eaten for a few days now. He's wasting away. I was wondering if you could get him some nutrition."

"Well, if he's not eating, we'll have to force-feed him. I'll check his charts, and if we can, we'll do it."

John probably wouldn't even notice an IV tube with all the other hospital paraphernalia. However, the doctor meant a tube up John's nose. I woke up the next morning to a vigorous phone message from John, though he hardly had a voice left.

"Hi, Susan! I'm wondering where you are, and why you told the doctor to feed me through a tube. I'll see you in the morning."

He had refused the tube, which made me strangely happy. He had exerted his will. He was still steering the ship. After John was gone, each time I listened to the recording, I smiled.

Pat and I met with a hospital social worker in the sunroom on John's floor, where she reviewed hospice options. I could not concentrate. A nearby hospice facility had an opening. I still thought that we hadn't tried everything we could to feed and hydrate John. Pat looked at me as though I might erupt or shatter.

"What do you think?" she asked after the social worker left. "My friend's mother was at that hospice. It's nice."

"I don't know." Why rush things? Why couldn't these bozos make John better?

Pat said, "Do you want to call Raegan and Kate?"

"Why?"

"They'll want to see him."

I agreed while privately dismissing Pat as an alarmist. Dust motes swirled in rays of sunlight, falling on the empty black vinyl chairs as we told Raegan and Kate that their dad wasn't getting better, and we were considering hospice. I felt like a traitor, giving him up. Time was racing and scrambling the narrative. I wanted the narrative back.

I filled out the paperwork for the hospice as though for John Doe, not for my husband. Raegan and Kate flew to Orlando the next day. When they walked into his room chattering away, John smiled through a semi-conscious drugged haze. He roused himself for them, just as he had over Christmas, and even ate a few bites of chocolate ice cream. I had to tell John that he was too sick now for the trial, and he would be moved to hospice the next day. He asked if he could go back to Pat's. We explained that he couldn't, but we would be with him. He took that in, and his glance skittered past me.

His eyes never opened again.

I would not be able to look into his eyes anymore and see the love there.

In the hospice, John had a large sunny yellow room with a lanai surrounded by a garden. The staff greeted us with cookies and flowers. The doctors and administrators explained that they would keep him comfortable and free from pain. A nurse told us that even if he did not respond when we spoke, he could hear us. Sound was the last sense to go.

As long as John breathed, I was not ready to let him go. But hour by hour, he left us:

Now here we are...John will be gone soon...this is too hard...

May he be free from pain, free from sorrow; may he know how much he is loved. I love him so.

Kate, Pat, and I took turns sitting on a chair next to the bed with him. While Kate and I talked quietly on the porch, birds chirped in the garden, and I glanced at Pat leaning toward John, whispering intently to the little brother she'd known all her life. I hope that she cracked a dark joke or two. He would have liked that.

I couldn't bear to look when Kate sat with him.

He was present, and yet his absence galloped toward us. His familiar, dear features subtly widened and sagged as death crept closer. I moistened his lips with a pink cherry medicated stick the nurse gave us. His chest rose and fell, and his thinning legs stiffened, sticking out of the blanket. I covered his feet, but a few seconds later, he shook the blanket off. Time slowed. Helpless, I sat next to him and stared. Over and over, I said, "I love you," though I'm not sure that I said it aloud.

On July 10th, 2016, the staff told us that John would pass away that day. His breathing grew fainter and more labored. At 9:50 p.m., the nurse placed a stethoscope on his heart, listened, shook her head, and tiptoed from the room. John was gone.

I hugged him and rubbed his head. He was still warm. I sobbed. It didn't make sense.

Reflecting on that day now, several years later, anger flares. He left too soon. I remember the night John's mother died of cancer while we were in our thirties and lived aboard *XL*. When John heard the news, he raced from dumpster to dumpster at the head of the dock and kicked each dumpster hard, his face distorted in fury. He ran through mud and puddles glistening under lurid yellow dock lights—smack, smack, smack. Then, his ferocity frightened me. Now, it comforts me.

We had been together for forty-four years.

It didn't feel like the end.

Chapter Twenty-Six
New Orleans

The sailor's knot par excellence, however, is the "Bow-line"...and wherever we find sailors, or seamen, we will find this knot in one or another of its various forms. When you can readily and surely tie this knot every time, you may feel yourself on the road to "Marline-spike Seamanship," for it is a true sailor's knot and never slips, jams, or fails; is easily and quickly untied; and is useful in a hundred places around boats or, in fact, in any walk of life.
—https://www.nps.gov/subjects/islandofthebluedolphins
/upload/Lesson-Plan-Sailors-Knots.pdf

The night John passed away, I slipped into bed in our room at Pat's house. *Our*: a possessive pronoun with which I had casually enveloped myself for forty-four years. We had stayed with Pat and Fred so often that they had named the guest room the Russell Room after us. Russell was John's last name. As I lay in bed, Kate popped in and asked if I wanted company.

"Yes," I said, and she climbed in on John's side.

"Do you snore?" she asked.

"I don't know!"

"Well, did Dad ever say you did?"

"Once or twice. He would poke me, and I stopped."

I woke up the next morning thinking I had to go to the hospice to see John, then I remembered. Flower arrangements arrived. A niece sent a link to Leon Russell's "A Song for You," and I played it over and over, picturing John and me on floor pillows around our hatch-cover table in Croton-on-Hudson, John's arm around me as we listened.

Kate prodded me along each day. Where was I going to live? The decision was easy now. I wanted to be near Kate in New Orleans. What kind of car did I want to buy? I had recently read a Stephen King mystery with an irascible, over-the-hill detective who drove a Prius. Kate helped me find a good deal, and I bought a sky-blue one.

We planned a memorial gathering on the water at a state park in Tampa. Kate made the arrangements and gathered stories from friends and relatives. We peeled out of The Villages for Tampa in the Prius, sun shining and rock n' roll blasting out of the open windows, distancing ourselves from the pain of the last few months.

That night in Tampa, Kate, Raegan, her children, Shae, and I found a tattoo parlor where a tattooist etched John's favorite knot, the bowline, on our arms. The bowline: the knot that always held, that John made me learn before we left on *Laughing Goat*. As the ink pierced the thin skin of my wrist, the unexpected pain lifted me out of the numbness creeping in.

At the park the next day, we pinned up photographs of John sailing, smoking, or lying in a hammock, alongside red and yellow Mexican party pennants that fluttered in the breeze. John's vitality bubbled through stories of relatives, friends, and business colleagues. I wasn't sure I could speak, but toward the end of the day, I said, "I never thought of myself as adventurous," to laughter.

As the day waned, a few of us tossed off our beach wraps and splashed into the water in our bathing suits. The late afternoon sun shone, and the water sparkled out to the horizon. John's spirit hovered in the fresh sea air.

In New Orleans, Kate drove me to an apartment I hoped to rent, an airy two stories in a pretty neighborhood near Audubon Park, with a porch and off-street parking. I put down a deposit.

The apartment would not be ready for two weeks. Alex's parents offered me their house for a week. The second week, Kate finessed a discount at a downtown hotel. I bought a new sunhat.

I wandered the French Quarter past Camilla's Grill, where John and I had gone for breakfast on an earlier trip. I roamed through bookstores and ate muffulettas at Central Grocery and beignets at Café du Monde as though I were on vacation. But as I peered in store windows in my new hat, my vacant smile stunned me. I felt as aimless as a feather. In my hotel room, I succumbed to delectable New Orleans food while sadness rolled in like the tide.

A friend of Kate's who had a flair for interior design shopped with me for furniture. Another friend's parent took me to an Al-Anon meeting. Someone else introduced me to her mother, who had just moved to New Orleans and had lost her husband, too.

Moving day arrived, and a lump tightened in my throat. I would no longer be in transit. Kate's friend, who had taken me shopping, borrowed a truck, and in the pouring rain, we picked up the chair and stools I had bought. With Kate and Alex, he then retrieved a couch, chest, and end tables from his mother, who was moving, too, and they moved everything into the apartment as rain drenched them. I didn't know how to express gratitude for such kindness, or for a daughter who marshaled her friends on my behalf.

I slept on a mattress on the floor. When I woke up in the morning and looked around at the mess, I cried. What was I doing here? I should have stayed in the uncluttered house in Merida and not listened to Kate's advice to come to New Orleans.

I gritted my teeth. I found my French press and brewed a cup of coffee. I cleaned and put my new armchair together. I bought pots and dishes at Target so I would have a functioning kitchen. The next day, I tackled the bed frame and box spring. I talked to John, who, I imagined, lauded my perseverance. Little by little, I fixed up the apartment.

I made plans each day. I attended Al-Anon meetings. I found a yoga class. I walked around Audubon Park with a new friend. I worked out at the gym. As I drove home from an activity, I would long for my bed. Exhaustion became my steadfast companion.

One day, I couldn't go out. I couldn't move. Leaning back on the couch with my eyes closed, my body shook. When we were first together, John would stand in front of me and count the seconds until I looked away from him. Then, I was so afraid of the strength of my feelings for him that I rarely looked into his eyes for more than a second. Now, my feelings spilled out, and I couldn't stop them.

On a trip to Merida to sort through our belongings, I visited my shrink-priest, who pointed out how John still sustained me. He gestured toward the bowline tattoo on my wrist—and reminded me that I still had Kate, who was so like John, and friends who provided love and support. He assured me that, over time, I would form a new relationship with the world. A sliver of hope gleamed. I walked to Plaza Grande and bought a Dairy Queen vanilla cone dipped in chocolate.

In the Mexico City airport on the way home, I spotted John just ahead of me, disappearing around a corner, hands in pockets, leaning forward as he had on the streets of New

York, and in line for coffee, and again, racing for the gate.

I had not realized the extent to which I left most decisions to John. As the days went by, I worked on that. My mantra became "WWJD—what would John do?"

Sadness and anger would lodge in my throat like an aching blob of mucus. My throat was so tight I could hardly speak— I made myself talk about it with friends who could listen. I took "gown days" when I didn't get out of my pajamas. I just allowed the misery in without fighting it.

Kate got engaged to Alex, who had secretly asked John for her hand when they visited Merida last Christmas. I shared Thanksgiving with Alex's family. In the weeks leading up to it, I announced that I would make John's key lime pie. But I could not rouse myself to buy the ingredients. As each day passed, it became clearer that I would not be able to make the pie, a reminder of his absence. I brought a fruit salad instead.

In my apartment, a red-and-purple Guatemalan pillow decorated my bed, and I'd draped a handwoven shawl John bought me in Chichicastenango, a Guatemalan village, on the headboard. Pictures of John and Kate filled the walls next to my bed. My favorite was of John in his twenties as we sailed on a friend's boat on Long Island Sound. Long blond hair blowing, a headband holding it off his face, broad, muscular back to the camera, he peered over his shoulder to check the wind.

I spent Christmas with Kate and Alex on his family's farm in Mississippi. After dinner on Christmas Eve, I turned in early. I tried to read, but the words swam. Kate poked her head in.

"What are you doing, Mom?"

"Reading. Thinking of Dad."

We hugged and cried—a good long cry. Holding her, it hurt a little less. Then we laughed, having trouble imagining John with us in rural Mississippi.

A week later, on New Year's Eve, I stayed in at my apartment. I had been invited to a party, but I wanted to be home. Over dessert—a slice of chocolate pie and a glass of wine—I watched a spy thriller on Netflix and surveyed my living room: fresh flowers, a watercolor of Kate at two, a photo of John lying in a hammock in Mexico without a care in the world, and a few prints of New Orleans. For a moment, I didn't ache.

"I think I'll be okay," I said aloud.

Chapter Twenty-Seven
Water

A few months after I moved to New Orleans, a friend invited me to go sailing. I accepted, but as the day neared, I obsessively checked the marine forecast for Lake Pontchartrain. My anxiety rose, and I knew I could not sail that day. Sailing, for me, was not a casual event. She asked me again, and eventually, I wanted to go. Kate came, too.

On the morning of the sail, I sat on my bed with John's foul weather jacket. I hadn't kept many of John's clothes, but I held onto his jacket. I stroked the stiff red folds and pressed it to my face, inhaling the sea tang—salt, and a tinge of mildew. In a pocket, I found a brass wood screw and a bent cotter pin. Closing my eyes, I pictured a flash of red as John slung the jacket on, slid his arms in the sleeves, and strode on deck to check the anchor line. I buried my head in the jacket and cried.

Sailing in New Orleans that day, our hosts asked if either of us wanted to take the helm. I hung back, not quite ready. Watching Kate steer, I remembered the easy camaraderie among John, Kate, and me when we sailed *Laughing Goat*.

Taking a turn later, I stood stiffly at the helm. My reverie of sailing on *Laughing Goat* vanished. But as the boat picked up speed, I relaxed. The boat responded like all the sailboats I had known with John—a quickening, sails fluttering and then filling, like a bird catching the wind and soaring.

John shared that feeling with me, the love of the moment when the boat, perfectly balanced, lets the wind take her. On the water that day, John's spirit was near.

When we plucked Kate out of second grade to sail off on *Laughing Goat*, I did not want to leave Fairfield.

I could have said no. *I could have said no.*

When we lived in Merida during what would be John's last year, I met a woman on the trip to Chiapas who had moved to Merida with her husband around the same time we had. She complained about contractors who didn't do what they were supposed to, and difficulties making real friends. I told her that John had cancer, and this was my first trip by myself. I lost myself in the Lacandon jungle, the waterfalls of Palenque, and the religious festivals in the mountains.

Brow furrowed, she said, "Is there anything you don't say yes to?" Perhaps she meant to disparage me, but I think she genuinely wanted to know.

I said yes to John, and each time I did, I learned something about myself.

Live on a ferryboat?

Sail away on *Laughing Goat*?

Move to Mexico while John had cancer?

Yes, yes, yes.

He didn't mind appearing ridiculous. He didn't care what people thought. He followed a through-line to the sea and to what was in his heart. He faced cancer as he would have faced a storm at sea, hunkering down, figuring out the best move, holding the boat—and us—together.

I said yes because, for me, it was the way forward.

John and Susan's wedding on *Phaedrus*, Stamford Harbor,
Connecticut, 1978

Laughing Goat, Isla Mujeres, Mexico, 1998

John, Kate, and Elmo on *Laughing Goat,* 1998

John on *Laughing Goat* in Warderick Wells, Exumas, 1997

Susan and Kate on *Laughing Goat* approaching Nassau, 1997

Susan, Kate, Shae and Olivia in Tampa, Florida, 2016

Acknowledgements

Deepest thanks to my generous, insightful readers: The Anarchist Book Club (Medora Monigold, Charly Borenstein-Regueira, Therese Close, Betsy Lody, Ann Roy), Shirly Lundy-Connor, Maggie Eber, Raegan Russell, Alex Reed, Janet Skiff, Lauren Kettler, Sarah Burkman, Pat Kuessner, Carolyn Healy, Barbara Evans, Marcella Prokop, Nancy Gentry, Claudia Barker, and Cy Bor.

Deepest gratitude to the outstanding instructors and staff of the Iowa Summer Writing Festival, especially my mentor, Sandra Scofield, without whom this book would not exist, and Marilyn Abildskov, an extraordinarily gifted teacher. Hope Edelman, Kim Vervaecke, Venise Berry, Sands Hall, Peter Trachtenberg, Mary Kay Shanley, Sarah Saffian and last but not least, Amy Margolis—thank you all for sharing your love of writing and nurturing mine.

I'm indebted to my wonderful publisher, Evelyn Byrne-Kusch of White Bird Publications, for taking a chance on me, and to her great team of editors for improving my prose; to all those who crossed paths with *Laughing Goat* and enriched our journey; to Cliff, who expertly guided us on longer passages; to family and friends who generously allowed me to include them in the book; and to so many who came into my life and lifted me up when I needed it—Dr. R., Father Jose, my magnificent New Orleans community, and my Fort Lauderdale walking buddies, to mention just a few.

Profound thanks to Maggie Eber who read every draft, faxed us in every port, sent Kate the latest nail polishes from the States, and kept all of our letters—had I dreamed up an imaginary ideal friend, it would be you; Alex, who pushed me to the finish line; Pat and Fred, who taught me what family means; Raegan, Shae, Olivia and Andrew, our bond forever cemented by a bowline tattoo; and my dad, who encouraged my childhood dreams and whose love sustains me still.

Most especially, thank you, Kate, for indulging your unconventional parents in a wild adventure, and making it your own. No one can make me laugh like you. I'm thrilled that Max will have the story of our voyage—at least, my version until yours comes along—to read someday.

John, you are always in my heart. We did it! This book is for you.

P.S. If you'd like to chat with the author and other memoir authors and readers, please consider joining the congenial Facebook group, We Love Memoirs.

Author's Note

I wrote *Holding Fast* from memory, notes in the ship's log, photographs, letters, faxes, emails and journal entries from the voyage. It is solely my perspective. Some names have been changed to protect privacy.